C. René Padilla and Lindy Scott

TERRORISM AND THE WAR IN IRAQ

A Christian Word from Latin America

Buenos Aires - 2004

Queda hecha el depósito que marca la ley 11.723

Impreso en Argentina
Printed in Argentina

www.kairos.org.ar

Padilla, Carlos René
    Terrorism and the War in Iraq : A Christian Word from
Latin America / Carlos René Padilla y Lindy Scott. – 1ª. ed. –
Buenos Aires : Kairós, 2004.
    186 p. ; 21x14 cm.

    ISBN 987-9403-68-1

    1. Terrorismo 2. Iraq-Guerra. I. Scott, Lindy II. Título
    CDD 303.625

In celebration of the thirtieth anniversary
of the International Congress on World Evangelization,
Lausanne, Switzerland,
16-25 July, 1974,
a historical world forum that laid down the basis
for a new way of looking at global Christianity

Contents

Contents

Preface

Terrorism and the War in Iraq: A Christian Word from Latin America is born out of the conviction that the followers of Jesus Christ are the Body of Christ and therefore have the challenge of representing Jesus on earth today. One aspect of that challenge is to interpret the important social events of our day in the light of God's Word and his concern for justice. This book strives to fulfill that calling by analyzing the current war in Iraq and terrorism in our world.

The subtitle *A Christian Word from Latin America* is significant. We are offering *a* word, not *the definitive* word. We do not claim infallibility, and we readily admit our limitations. Nevertheless, we desire that this volume be a stimulus to further discussion on the issues involved. We desire to present a *Christian word* on the war and terrorism, with insights from Scripture and Christian teaching. We are disturbed that there has been very little analysis of the war and terrorism by churches in the United States, although our God surely is not indifferent to the events taking place in Iraq and throughout the world. God has something to say about wars and terrorism in our world today, and we humbly desire to understand his thoughts. We also recognize that we bring a Christian word *from Latin America*. We believe that the Body of Christ extends all over the world. No member of that Body can be healthy if it is separated from the rest of the Body. Given the natural human tendency towards ethnocentrism we all need to receive constructive criticism from those who love us and see us from a different vantage point.

Christians in Latin America desire both to give and to receive that necessary, life-giving, constructive criticism.

During the first few months of 2003 a wide variety of Latin American churches and Christian organizations issued formal statements regarding the war in Iraq. The first chapter documents those pronouncements in detail.

God calls all of his children to be salt and light in this needy world. We dare not shy away from the tough ethical decisions that must be made in order to fulfill this vocation. The taking of life and the protection of life are serious matters, and we affirm that God's Word provides us with moral insight regarding these matters. God calls his children to be peacemakers. Down through the ages, Christians have disagreed on the best way to pursue that peace. While some Christians believe that pacifism is the best way to follow Jesus, others believe that, under certain circumstances, the best way to achieve peace is through a "just war." Without necessarily advocating ourselves the "just war theory," in the second chapter we evaluate the war in Iraq according to the seven generally accepted criteria of this theory.

Intervention by one country in the affairs of another is not a new phenomenon. Much can be learned from studying the history of these interventions. Chapter three looks at the United States' intervention in Iraq in light of previous U.S. interventions in Latin America and the Caribbean.

The fourth chapter looks at the effects of materialism and hyper-patriotism upon both the church and the culture in the United States. Scripture links these two "isms" to idolatry. They frequently are depicted as having a pernicious effect upon the lives of Christians and the testimony of the church.

The last chapter provides suggestions on how to proceed from an unjust war to a more just peace in Iraq and throughout the world. We outline a different vision for the role of the United States in the world. We also suggest steps that we Christians need to take in order to be more faithful followers of our Lord in the twenty-first century.

The first appendix is a simple yet passionate letter from Pastor Jorge Galli, a Baptist minister in Buenos Aires, Argentina. His words are addressed to North American Christians regarding the war. They were first presented in person in Buenos Aires to students and professors from Wheaton College and Houston Baptist University in the summer of 2003. His gentle spirit combined with his straight talk had a deep impact upon the teachers and students alike. We believe that a larger Christian audience in the United States would also benefit from his thoughts.

The second appendix, entitled "Theology and Implications of Radical Discipleship," is a historical document drawn up by an *ad hoc* group of about four hundred "young evangelicals" that met spontaneously during the memorable International Congress on World Evangelization, which took place in Lausanne, Switzerland, July 16-25, 1974. Its purpose was to underline the inextricable unity that there is between discipleship and the multifaceted mission of the Church. Issued at the end of the Congress, together with *The Lausanne Covenant,* it was signed by a high number of the participants. Although it had a rather limited circulation, it may be regarded as the first world-wide evangelical statement on holistic mission.

We appreciate the many friends, too numerous to mention, who have helped shape this book with their comments and constructive criticism. Our special gratitude goes out to Arthur Holmes for his suggestions on the second chapter. We are especially thankful for Gretchen Gaither and Catharine Padilla for their excellent editorial work. Nevertheless, we alone are responsible for the final edition.

   In this book we are not questioning the sincerity of the soldiers who are fighting in the war (soldiers fighting for the coalition forces as well as those on the other side waging urban guerrilla warfare against those troops). Nevertheless, we must go beyond sincerity and good intentions. Actions as well as attitudes must be evaluated according to God's high moral standards as presented in His Word. It is our wish that this modest book contribute to greater faithfulness on the part of those who call on the name of the Lord.

C. René Padilla and Lindy Scott
August 2004

1

The War in Iraq: The Latin American Churches Speak Out

So in Christ we who are many form one body,
and each member belongs to all the others.
(Romans 12:5)

And if one member suffers, all the members suffer with it;
if one member is honored, all the members rejoice with it.
(I Corinthians 12:26)

The invasion of Iraq in March 2003 by the armed forces of the United States, Great Britain, and a few allies provoked a great polarization in our world. The overwhelming majority of demonstrations outside the United States were protests against the war. Although there were large protests within the United States as well, surveys revealed that leading up to the invasion North Americans were fairly evenly divided, in favor and against the war. Once the bombs began to fall, the percentage of North Americans who supported the war rose to 70% or even higher.

This chapter narrates how various Protestant churches and organizations in Latin America responded to this war. As a backdrop it should be mentioned that some denominations in the United States (mostly "mainline" denominations and the Roman

Catholic Church) officially came out against the war. But at the level of the "person in the pew," patriotic support for "the President and our troops" was quite strong. Support from the "evangelical" wing of United States Protestantism was even higher, probably above 80%.

Latin American Protestants and the War

How did Protestants in Latin America respond? Three major options seemed possible. The first option presupposed that, given the historical relationship between Latin American Protestants and their counterparts (missionaries, literature, funding, etc.) in the United States, it would seem plausible that Latin American Protestants would support the war. Perhaps even more likely was the possibility that the Latin American churches would remain silent on the issue, typical of their *apolitical* posture throughout much of the twentieth century.[1] Lastly, given the fact that Latin Americans in general were quite against the war, it was possible that the Latin American churches would also take a public stand against the war.

This third option is, indeed, the one that was chosen. What is surprising is that the overwhelming majority of Latin American churches that took a public position regarding the war strongly

---

[1] For a good overall view of this "apolitical" stance see C. René Padilla, ed., *De la marginación al compromiso: Los evangélicos y la política en América Latina*. Buenos Aires: Fraternidad Teológica Latinoamericana, 1991. For a more detailed study of this posture in Mexico see Scott, *Salt of the Earth: A Socio-Political History of Mexico City Evangelical Protestants (1964-1991)*. Mexico City: Editorial Kyrios, 1991.

denounced it, and they based their denunciations primarily on moral grounds. Most of the critiques of the war dealt with the first four criteria of the Just War theory.[2]

Although there is a long tradition of pacifism within the history of Christianity, the more dominant position, especially since Constantine, has been the theory of the Just War. According to this theory, although all Christians are called to be peacemakers, in a few circumstances it might be necessary to use limited warfare to avoid greater bloodshed. Nevertheless, Christians should not participate in wars unless all seven criteria of the Just War theory have been fulfilled. These criteria are (1) just cause; (2) just intention; (3) last resort; (4) formal declaration; (5) limited objectives; (6) proportionate means; and (7) noncombatant immunity.[3]

It could be anticipated that the churches affiliated with the *Consejo Latinoamericano de Iglesias* (an association of churches in Latin America with ties to the World Council of Churches) would denounce the war, because in the past it has criticized the foreign policies of the United States. Nevertheless, it was not so readily expected that conservative churches and "apolitical" churches would do the same. The examples that follow are merely a sample of their pronouncements.

The Executive National Committee of the *Unión Evangélica Pentecostal Venezolana* (Venezuelan Evangelical Pentecostal Union) sent a pastoral letter to all of their member churches

---

[2] The second chapter of this book analyzes in greater detail the war in Iraq in the light of Just War criteria.

[3] These criteria have been clearly articulated by Arthur Holmes in Robert G. Clouse, ed., *War: Four Christian Views*. Downers Grove, IL: InterVarsity Press, 1981, pp. 117-135.

expressing their "rejection of the war that is currently being waged in Iraq and of the world war project that the great centers of world power are orchestrating."[4] Consequently the pentecostal leaders "urge the governments of the United States, England and Spain to heed the voices that are raised everywhere in opposition to the war, because it does not guarantee the well-being nor the security of any person or nation."[5]

The Executive Committee of the *Fraternidad Teológica Latinoamericana* (Latin American Theological Fraternity) strongly denounced the war and declared it to be "illegal, immoral and inhumane."[6] The declaration accused the United States and Great Britain of having supported the despot Saddam Hussein for decades and now waging war against him in an invasion that attempted to hide their economic interests. The true motives of the war were connected to a similar penetration in Latin America such as the *Plan Pueblo-Panamá*, the *Plan Colombia* and the *ALCA*. In addition to all the immoralities of the war, it would also have negative effects on evangelism, because "the havoc wreaked by two 'Christian' nations would invalidate the proclamation of the gospel in cultures whose voices and contributions we have not yet listened to nor appreciated."[7]

One of the most surprising denunciations of the war came from the Baptist World Alliance. While some prominent Baptists

---

[4] *"Iglesias pentecostales rechazan la guerra y llaman a participar en los cambios del país"* in *Servicio de Noticias ALC*: March 25, 2003.

[5] Ibid.

[6] President Lilia Solano Góngora, *"Comunicado de la Fraternidad Teológica Latinoamericana sobre la guerra."* Fraternidad Teológica Latinoamericana: March 24, 2003.

[7] Ibid.

in the United States came out in support of the war, the Baptist World Alliance with strong influence from its Latin American members condemned the invasion as "a great sin." In the capital, Washington D.C., the Alliance declared that "war is always a failure of humanity to achieve the will of God for peace."[8]

The *Red Latinoamericana de Abogados Cristianos* (*RLAC*, Latin American Network of Christian Lawyers), consisting of more than 100 legal professionals from 14 Latin American countries, expressed "their most profound rejection of this illegitimate military intervention."[9] As could be expected, this legal association protested the violations against international law and against its democratic foundations. They denounced the hypocrisy of the Bush administration for "the way that the North American government has manipulated democratic values and, under the guise of democracy, it would sacrifice innocent Iraqi men, women and children, in the quest of economic and geopolitical interests."[10] They accused the United States of a moral "double standard" by attacking a nation without following the appropriate channels established by the Magna Carta of the United Nations.

The *Foro Ecuménico por la Paz y la Reconciliación* (Ecumenical Forum for Peace and Reconciliation, Guatemala) groups together the Episcopal, Presbyterian, Guatemalan Lutheran, and *Cristo Rey* Lutheran Protestant Churches, the Conference of Guatemalan Evangelical Churches (*Conferencia*

---

[8] "*Fraternidad Teológica Latinoamericana y Alianza Bautista Mundial rechazan la guerra*" en *Servicio de Noticias ALC*: March 25, 2003.

[9] "*Abogados cristianos condenan la guerra en Irak*" in *Servicio de Noticias ALC*: March 26, 2003.

[10] Ibid.

de Iglesias Evangélicas de Guatemala or *CIEDEG*), in addition to
the Ecumenical and Theological Commission of the Roman
Catholic Bishops Conference (*La Comisión de Ecumenismo y
Teología de la Conferencia Episcopal*), the Conference of
Religious Orders and the Orthodox Church Community. This
Ecumenical Forum denounced the United States' invasion of Iraq
and unmasked the motivations used to justify the war. "Wars are
unnecessary and do not coincide with the ethical and moral
values of our societies; only those cultures and people that
promote relationships of unequal, asymmetrical power,
competition, mistrust, fears, frustrations, and threats *justify wars
in order to maintain their position.*"[11] The pronouncement
alluded to passages in the Old Testament where "God is our
reason for hope, as the strength of life and guarantee of peace for
the future of men and women." People must therefore reject the
use of armed conflict. The document urged the Guatemalan
people to "express themselves in favor of peace and to commit
themselves to never lose sight of the Guatemalan peace
process."[12] On March 30 the Evangelical Conference carried out
a liturgical ceremony that brought together leaders and members
of the Mennonite, Kaqchikel Presbyterian, Catholic, Pentecostal,
Central American, and Orthodox churches, in which David Son,
Executive Secretary of the CIEDEG, extended an exhortation to
Bush and Blair to reconsider their actions: "The powerful act out
of evil when they fuel war. We hope that those who push a

---

[11] Antonio Otzoy, *"Foro Ecuménico se suma a clamor mundial y pide
cese de ataque a Irak"* in *Servicio de Noticias ALC*: April 4, 2003,
(emphasis mine).

[12] Ibid.

button to destroy might have a moment of reflection about the impact of their actions that cut short human life."[13]

The *Universidad Politécnica de Nicaragua* (*UPOLI*, the Polytechnic University of Nicaragua) is sponsored by the Baptist Church in Nicaragua. During the first days of April 2003, students from the university presented an exhibition showing the effects of the missiles and bombs that were falling upon Iraq. Titled "When the Powerful Believe Themselves to be Gods," the exposition denounced the war unleashed by the governments of the United States and England and the suffering caused to children, to the hungry, to the disinherited and to those who were being used as human shields. María del Socorro Rodríguez, professor of the University, stated, "The war against Iraq violates international law. I do not want to be an accomplice, by my silence, to an action that undermines the foundations of world peace."[14] The Palestinian ambassador to Nicaragua, George Solama, addressed the students and discredited Bush's argument regarding the weapons of mass destruction that Saddam Hussein supposedly possessed. The diplomat affirmed, "Saddam Hussein is not a danger for international security nor for peace, because he does not possess chemical nor biological weapons, nor relations with terrorist organizations."[15] He affirmed that the true motivation for the invasion was oil and the concomitant control of the Middle East. Hundreds of university students and professors responded to the exhibition with fasting and prayer vigils on behalf of world peace.

---

[13] Ibid.

[14] Trinidad Vásquez, *"Universitarios presentan exposición 'Cuando los poderosos se creen dioses'"* in *Servicio de Noticias ALC*: April 4, 2003.

[15] Ibid.

The Latin American and Caribbean Pre-Assembly of the World Lutheran Federation met in San Salvador, El Salvador, during April 6-9, 2003. Delegates took advantage of their meeting to pronounce a prophetic word regarding the war. In the inaugural address, Brazilian theologian Walter Altmann connected his comments on the war with the general theme of the assembly: "The holistic healing of the world." He affirmed that "with much fewer resources than those spent in the war we could solve problems like world hunger and other acute needs...the war will have an extremely high human and social cost, not only in civilian deaths, especially children, but also due to the destruction of basic resources for the survival of the people."[16] His predictions are sadly coming true.[17] Altmann foresaw tragic consequences for the relations between religions, particularly between Islam and Christianity, because "Bush (just like Saddam Hussein) insists on invoking the blessing of God upon his bellicose action." In the same assembly, Ismael Noko, the General Secretary of the World Lutheran Federation, repeated a condemnation of the war as unjustifiable for having violated international ethical norms. Noko, with eerie accuracy, predicted that "the United States and Great Britain will win the war, but will lose the peace" and "with this attack the anti-U.S. sentiment will deepen throughout the world and will provoke greater tensions between Christian and Muslim communities."[18]

---

[16] "*Walter Altmann pronunció discurso inaugural de pre-asamblea luterana*" in *Servicio de Noticias ALC*: April 6, 2003.

[17] The accuracy of his prediction is seen in the cost of the war in Iraq and the following reconstruction. It has risen to $166,000,000,000.00 during the first 16 months and it continues to rise.

[18] "*El secretario general de la Federación Luterana reafirma rechazo a guerra contra Irak*" in *Servicio de Noticias ALC*: April 7, 2003.

On April 10, Federico Pagura, Bishop Emeritus of the Argentine Methodist Church, denounced the war of the United States and its allies against Iraq and called it a "genocidal invasion" against the Iraqi people. He condemned the hypocrisy of the United States for having initiated this aggression "with the pretext of overthrowing Saddam Hussein who, like other dictators around the world, has been created and/or maintained by administrations of *the same imperial colossus of the North.*"[19] Pagura identified the United States as "the number one terrorist power on earth." He joined other Latin American evangelical leaders (such as the ex-president of the *Universidad Bíblica Latinoamericana* in Costa Rica, Elsa Támez) in his commitment to not traveling to the United States as a personal protest.

Mexico

Mexican Protestants also announced their repudiation of the war. A wide spectrum of seminaries, including the Anglicans, the Baptists, the Lutherans, the Methodists, the Presbyterians and the influential *Comunidad Teológica de México*, plus the Berea, Elim and Anabaptist Bible Institutes, came together to publish a joint declaration in which they affirmed, "we join our voice to the official voice of various Christian entities throughout the world and in Mexico that have declared to be against the war" and "we declare ourselves to be against the official posture of the governments of the United States, Great Britain and Spain who

---

[19] *"Obispo Pagura adhiere a las protestas contra la guerra en Irak"* in *Servicio de Noticias ALC*: April 10, 2003, (emphasis mine).

in the name of God are invading Iraq."[20] They later insinuated that Bush and his allies practice idolatry because they serve another god. "This is not the God that we know. The One that we know is the God of history and therefore, the One that demands justice, peace and love. This is the God that is revealed in Jesus Christ, who opens opportunities for life, for inclusiveness, and for solidarity. It is the God who calls us to be peacemakers in the construction of a new earth."[21]

One of the most surprising declarations came from the National Presbyterian Church of Mexico (INPM). In their official magazine, *El Faro*, the Presbyterians condemned the war against Iraq in no uncertain terms. The title itself "La *Iglesia Nacional Presbiteriana de México* se une a la Alianza Reformada de Iglesias *y condena la guerra contra Irak*" (The National Presbyterian Church of Mexico joins with the Alliance of Reformed Churches to Condemn the War against Iraq) expressed their passionate cry against the war.[22]

The declaration begins with "profound sadness and sorrow" because "the force of international opinion was not able in the last instance to dissuade the government of the United States and the few allies that followed it from launching a war that will bring about suffering, misery and death for thousands of Iraqis and perhaps many other people from other places."[23] The article

---

[20] "*Evangélicos de México, Argentina y Perú también están por la paz*" in *Servicio de Noticias ALC*: April 2, 2003.

[21] Ibid.

[22] President Jorge López Pérez, "La *Iglesia Nacional Presbiteriana de México se une a la Alianza Reformada de Iglesias y condena la Guerra contra Irak*" in *El Faro* (May-June 2003): 35 (original emphasis).

[23] Ibid.

denounces this war begun without the authorization of the United Nations as *"immoral* and *illegal.* And utilizing a term that is traditional to us, it is a *sin."*[24] Therefore, "we Presbyterians categorically condemn the war for the unilateral and imperialistic mentality upon which it is based. No nation, however powerful it may be, can act upon the world scene just as it wishes."[25] The article later refers to President Bush. It alludes to his affirmation that the people of the world have to be *in favor of* or *against* the United States. "A unipolar world, in which a superpower offers us the option of being with it or against it is an unacceptable world from a moral and political point of view. President Bush and his administration need to remember that *the evangelical option is to be in favor of or against Christ."*[26] Bush's affirmation came so close to blasphemy that many Latin American Christians identified the United States' connection between faith and patriotism as "Yankee syncretism."

Later, the article criticizes the government of the United States for utilizing anti-democratic methods in the United Nations. "We congratulate the majority of the countries represented on the United Nations Security Council and especially our country for not allowing themselves to be *hounded, bribed,* or *intimidated* to the point of supporting the war. We call upon the General Assembly of the United Nations to discuss at the earliest possible moment this reckless affront to international law."[27]

The article ends with various exhortations: one to the people of the world and to their governments to "reaffirm the authority

---

[24] Ibid (emphasis mine).

[25] Ibid.

[26] Ibid (emphasis mine).

[27] Ibid (emphasis mine).

of the United Nations." The second exhortation is addressed to the aggressor states, demanding that "they immediately stop their attacks." The final exhortation is for the church to "pray and make its voices of protest heard."

This declaration of the Mexican Presbyterian Church is surprising due to the denomination's own history in the political realm. In its beginnings, the Presbyterian Church had been quite active in Mexican politics. Nevertheless, beginning in the 1930s the Presbyterians entered into a period in which they strove to become "apolitical."[28] In Mexico, the Presbyterians are known as one of the most conservative denominations, especially with regard to socio-political issues. In 1972 the denomination broke off official ties with Presbyterians in the United States because they were "too liberal." More recently, Mexican Presbyterians have strengthened connections with the Presbyterian Church of America (PCA), one of the more conservative denominations in the United States. This declaration of the Mexican Presbyterians went against the sentiments of many of their fellow Presbyterians in the United States.

Later Events

In recent months several churches have continued their pronouncements regarding the situation in Iraq. In the first days of September 2003, the Salvadoran Lutheran Synod made a declaration against the sending of Salvadoran troops to participate with the occupation forces in Iraq. The situation in Iraq is "extremely dangerous" for the 380 Salvadoran soldiers

---

[28] See the chapter on the *National Presbyterian Church of Mexico* in Scott, *Salt of the Earth*, pp. 49-76.

who are located there.[29] Their declaration made reference to the fact that El Salvador, as a member of the United Nations and as a signer of the Chapultepec Peace Accords (1992), committed itself to work for peace and reconciliation. Having intimately known war, our people "reject war." Bishop Medardo Gómez asked for the annulment of the legislative decree that authorized the sending of troops to Iraq. He argued that it was illegal because El Salvador had not declared war upon Iraq.

In September of 2003, the Micah Network brought together 185 evangelical leaders from more than 50 countries in Querétaro, Mexico, to discuss the theme of globalization from a Christian perspective. Although the war in Iraq was not a part of the original schedule, the delegates recognized the necessity to deal with it. The final declaration expressed that the International Court must be strengthened so that it could better judge cases of international wars. It demanded that the United Nations be supported with greater finances so that it would be able to better carry out its functions. It also denounced the use of "terrorism" as a pretext for wars, when 30,000 persons die every day due to hunger and illnesses.[30]

Church leaders in Ecuador[31] and Argentina have publicly stated that the presence of certain evangelical leaders from the United States would be counterproductive to the proclamation of the gospel in their countries. The clearest example has to do with

---

[29] "*Luteranos contra el envío de tropas salvadoreñas a Irak*" in *Servicio de Noticias ALC*: September 1, 2003.

[30] "*La Declaración de Querétaro: La Globalización y los Pobres*". Querétaro: Red Miqueas (Micah Network), 2003.

[31] The Ecuadorian response can be found at http://www.protestante digital.com/hemeroteca/006/index.htm.

evangelist Franklin Graham (son of famous evangelist Billy Graham). The younger Graham was scheduled to give evangelistic messages in Rosario, Argentina, in November 2003, at the "Festival of Hope." The Kairos Community, with the support of the *Fraternidad Teológica Latinoamericana* (Buenos Aires chapter), wrote that the participation of Graham in this evangelical event constituted "an ethical problem of great magnitude, if we keep in mind that Franklin Graham is a religious advisor to George W. Bush, and is frankly offensive, among other reasons, for the explicit support that the preacher gave to the invasion of Iraq by the United States."[32] The Argentine document continued: "While almost the entire world, including many Argentine men and women, perceive the bellicose actions of the governments of George Bush and Tony Blair as a criminal act, how can we Argentine evangelicals give a welcome to someone who has contributed to the utilization of our faith to justify such an act?"[33]

Observations

It has been a surprise to many observers to see the unanimity of these pronouncements. Every single one condemned the war as immoral. We are not aware of any denomination in Latin America that came out in favor of the war. An article in one pentecostal magazine did see the war as fitting into God's eschatological plan, but even this article did not favor the war.

---

[32] "*Fundación Evangélica Kairós rechaza presentación del predicador Franklin Graham*" in *Servicio de Noticias ALC*: November 4, 2003.

[33] Ibid.

Although Protestant churches, especially the ones that made the declarations, are historically democratic, in general it was their leaders who denounced the war in the name of (and not necessarily consulting with) their members. Perhaps this is the rise of the *"profeta evangélico"* (evangelical prophet) or *"cacique religioso* (religious chief)." It is to be expected that Latin American Protestant leaders will make more of these types of pronouncements in the future.

These Latin American churches, at least in symbolic ways, are further severing the umbilical cord with the churches in the United States. Many evangelical leaders in Latin America have rejected the priorities of churches in the North.[34] It is likely that the Latin American churches will distance themselves even further from their "spiritual parents" in the north.

---

[34] It is illuminating to see the critique of North American churches by Brazilian Assembly of God pastor Ricardo Gondim in *"Pastor cuestiona la importación de modelos evangélicos"* in *Servicios de Noticias ALC*: November 1, 2002. It is important to point out that Gondim had studied in the United States but now rejects what he considers to be non-Biblical alliances that United States evangelicals have formed. His critique included the following: "North American evangelicals sympathize with the Republican Party, venerate their president and believe that the future of their country is tied to prayer in school, prohibition of abortion, and the denunciation of homosexuality...they are not very interested in the emission of toxic gases into the atmosphere, the AIDS epidemic in Africa, or the inequality of commercial relations with the poor countries of our planet." Gondim continued his critique of Protestant preaching in the United States: "You never hear from North American pulpits any denunciation of the tariffs on imports or subsidies of their agricultural products that affect the economies of poor nations. The 'American way of life' and the gospel are Siamese twins. It is almost impossible to separate them."

Many of the denominations and organizations made declarations that aligned with the posture of their own international ecclesiastical body, for example the World Baptist Alliance, the World Lutheran Federation or the Alliance of Reformed Churches. Many of their critiques pointed out how the United States did not follow the appropriate channels laid out by the United Nations and "went it alone." These denominations were careful not to commit the same mistake, because they frequently connected their pronouncements with those of their international associations.

In general, the Latin American evangelical protests lined up with the posture of their own national governments and the sentiments of their own people. It is possible to interpret these denunciations as the Latin American expression of "evangelical patriotism." Nevertheless, there are indications of rising prophetic voices that do challenge the position of national governments (for example, the Lutherans in El Salvador). When church pronouncements and national positions do coincide, a good dose of suspicion is in order. Nevertheless, the essential issue is the content of the argument raised, not its agreement (nor disagreement) with the national position. These denunciations might very well be valid and helpful observations from another perspective.

The invasion of Iraq by the United States and England has raised great interest again in political ethics and the role of churches in modern societies. Latin American churches have begun making their voices heard. Their articulate pronouncements are making a contribution to the ethical debate needed in our contemporary world. In the next chapter we will heed their exhortation and examine the war in Iraq in light of Christian teaching.

2

The War in Iraq: How Just was this War?

Woe to those who call evil good and good evil.
(Isaiah 5:20)

The kings of the Gentiles lord it over them;
and those who exercise authority over them call themselves Benefactors.
(Luke 22:25)

Jesus calls all of his followers to be peacemakers (Matthew 5:9). There is no doubt regarding that charge. Nevertheless, there is disagreement regarding how Christians should strive to promote that peace. For the first three hundred years in the life of the church, many Christians were pacifists. They believed that the use of violence would be a denial of their obedience to the Lord Jesus. With Constantine and the privileges that he granted to the church, the followers of Jesus began to face a new challenge. What should Christians do when their "Christian" government asked or ordered them to take up arms and fight a national enemy? Some Christians came to the belief that under certain circumstances it would be acceptable to fight in a war. As evangelical historian Ronald Wells clarifies,

> Christians borrowed models of behavior about war from Jewish and classical cultures.... Thus the "Christian" ethic of war that emerged after the fourth century was not

distinctly Christian, but rather was based on Hebrew, Greek, and especially Roman ethics, accommodated to the needs of a "Christian culture."[1]

Over the following centuries theologians struggled to sharpen the criteria that would constitute a "just war." Most just war theoreticians today agree that there are seven essential criteria that must be met if a war can be considered justified. In contrast with this belief, a significant portion of the church has continued to be pacifist (denominations like the Mennonites, the Quakers, certain Brethren groups, and many followers of Jesus within other Christian denominations).

For the sake of argument, in this chapter it will be assumed that the "Just War Theory" is a valid Christian position. The participation of Christians in wars can be justified, but *only if all seven "just war" criteria are met*. On the following pages the war in Iraq will be evaluated according to these criteria. One of the clearest presentations of the Just War theory has been articulated by Arthur Holmes, eminent evangelical philosopher and Wheaton College Professor Emeritus.[2] According to Holmes, all of the following criteria must be fulfilled for Christian participation in a war to be considered acceptable behavior:

---

[1] Ronald A. Wells, ed., *The Wars of America: Christian Views*. Grand Rapids: Eerdmans, 1981, p. 7. Christian ethicist Paul Ramsey gives a more sympathetic view of this process, claiming that Augustine reworked the Roman ethic of war in light of the Christian ethic of love.

[2] A very succinct presentation can be found in Arthur F. Holmes, "The Just War" in Robert G. Clouse, ed. *War: Four Christian Views*. Downers Grove: InterVarsity Press, 1981, pp. 117-135. An added quality of this book is that four eminent Christian scholars present their own views and then critique the positions of their colleagues.

1. **Just cause**. All aggression is condemned; only defensive war is legitimate.
2. **Just intention**. The only legitimate intention is to secure a just peace for all involved. Neither revenge nor conquest nor economic gain nor ideological supremacy are justified.
3. **Last resort**. War may only be entered upon when all negotiations and compromise have been tried and have failed.
4. **Formal declaration**. Since the use of military force is the prerogative of governments, not of private individuals, a state of war must be officially declared by the highest authorities.
5. **Limited objectives**. If the purpose is peace, then unconditional surrender or the destruction of a nation's economic or political institutions is an unwarranted objective.
6. **Proportionate means**. The weaponry and the force used should be limited to what is needed to repel the aggression and deter future attacks, that is to say, to secure a just peace. Total or unlimited war is ruled out.
7. **Noncombatant immunity**. Since war is an official act of government, only those who are officially agents of government may fight, and individuals not actively contributing to the conflict (including POWs and casualties as well as civilian nonparticipants) should be immune from attack.[3]

Now let us turn to the war in Iraq and evaluate it according to these principles. Readers are encouraged to examine the

---

[3] Holmes, "The Just War," pp. 120-121. Some scholars, like Yoder, *When War is Unjust*, p. 18, suggest an additional criterion: the probability of success, which requires accurate estimates prior to engaging in war. Instead of treating this as a separate criterion, we will incorporate it into the discussion of the other criteria, where appropriate.

evidence as rigorously as possible and, thereby, to express their love for the Lord with all their minds.

Just Cause

Three main arguments were put forth by the Bush administration claiming that a war against Iraq had a justified cause. The first allegation was that Saddam Hussein was a terrorist with ties to the attacks carried out on the World Trade Center and the Pentagon by Al Qaeda on September 11, 2001. The second claim was that Saddam Hussein possessed and would use weapons of mass destruction. The third was that Saddam Hussein was a tyrant who had committed genocide and other atrocities against his own people. We will look at each of these allegations in turn.

I. The Bush administration repeatedly urged war against Iraq because Saddam Hussein was a terrorist. The terrorist attacks of September 11, 2001 rightfully worried the U.S. public. "The war on terror" became a favorite phrase of the media. The Bush administration frequently asserted that Saddam Hussein was a key figure in world terrorism. In his oft-quoted "axis of evil" State of the Union address in January 2002, President Bush claimed that Iraq, Iran and North Korea, together with their "terrorist allies, constitute an axis of evil, arming to threaten the peace of the world."[4]

Top administration officials repeatedly made statements associating Saddam Hussein's regime with the September 11 attacks. Defense Secretary Donald Rumsfeld affirmed, "There

---

[4] President Bush's State of the Union Address, January 2002.

are Al Qaeda in Iraq." National Security Adviser Condoleezza Rice proclaimed, "Saddam Hussein cavorts with terrorists." President Bush repeated the accusation: "The [Iraqi] regime has longstanding and continuing ties to terrorist organizations and there are Al Qaeda terrorists inside Iraq." Key Democratic leaders, such as Hillary Rodham Clinton and Tom Daschle, also argued in favor of going to war against Iraq because Saddam Hussein had supposedly collaborated with Al Qaeda in the September 11 attacks.[5]

In his infamous speech aboard the *USS Abraham Lincoln* aircraft carrier on May 1, 2003, announcing the end to major combat in Iraq, Bush continued the same argument connecting Iraq and 9/11. *"The battle of Iraq is one victory in a war on terror that began on Sept. 11, 2001*—and still goes on." He then added that the victory over Iraq had "removed *an ally of Al Qaeda*." He further expanded on the connection by saying, "With those attacks" on September 11, "the terrorists and their supporters declared war on the United States. And war is what they got."[6]

These statements coming out of the administration had their desired effect. A poll (taken in September, 2003) revealed that 70% of U. S. Americans believed that Saddam Hussein was involved in the September 11 attacks. When asked about that

---

[5] "Should the Senate Approve H.J. Res. 114, to Authorize the Use of Military Force Against Iraq? - PRO - Sen. Hillary Rodham Clinton (NY-D) *Congressional Digest.* 81, no. 10, (2002): 314 and "Should the Senate Approve H.J. Res. 114, to Authorize the Use of Military Force Against Iraq? - PRO - Sen. Tom Daschle (SD-D) *Congressional Digest.* 81, no. 10, (2002): 306-309.

[6] Bob Kemper, "Bush: No Iraqi link to Sept. 11" in the *Chicago Tribune*, September 18, 2003, p. 6.

poll on the *Meet the Press* television news program, Vice President Cheney responded, "I think it's not surprising that people make that connection." Cheney then elaborated, "If we're successful in Iraq... then we will have struck a major blow right at the heart of the base, if you will, *the geographical base of the terrorists who have had us under assault for many years, but most especially on 9/11.*"[7]

Reporters doggedly questioned President Bush to see if he would back up the Vice President's remarks connecting Iraq and the 9/11 attacks. Knowing that the evidence just did not exist, Bush had to back away from both Cheney's remark and from the public perception that his own administration had cultivated. Bush finally made his confession, *"We've had no evidence that Saddam Hussein was involved with Sept. 11."*[8]

Ray McGovern, a CIA analyst with 27 years of service, expressed a common sentiment within the CIA regarding the alleged Iraq-Al Qaeda connection.

> The ties with Al Qaeda was just a scare tactic to exploit the trauma, the very real trauma, that the American people have felt ever since 9/11 and to associate that trauma with Iraq. As you know from the polls, most Americans believed that Iraq had something to do with 9/11, and that was a very successful, very deliberate and *very unethical* and *immoral* operation on the part of the P.R. people of this administration.[9]

Mel Goodman, Senior CIA analyst for twenty years, expressed a similar opinion, "Iraq... was not part of the picture

---

[7] Ibid., p. 1.
[8] Ibid.
[9] *Uncovered: The Whole Truth about the Iraq War*, 2003, (video).

of terrorism before we invaded; Saddam Hussein and Bin Laden were enemies."[10]

Charles Freeman, former United States ambassador to Saudi Arabia during the first Gulf War and with thirty years of diplomatic service concurred, "...*the war really had absolutely nothing to do with terrorism, there was no connection whatsoever between Iraq and the secular regime there and the religious fanatics who perpetrated 9/11.*"[11]

Months after President Bush admitted there was no connection between Saddam Hussein and Al Qaeda, the administration continued to circulate the claim that there was such a connection. In an interview on January 9, 2004, Vice President Cheney affirmed, "There's overwhelming evidence there was a connection between Al Qaeda and the Iraqi government. I am very confident that there was an established relationship there."[12] Cheney based his claim upon a document analyzed by the Department of Defense and forwarded to the Senate Intelligence Committee. What the Vice President "forgot" to mention was that the Defense Department itself had declared the document "inaccurate" when it was published.

As late as June 14, 2004, Vice President Cheney again repeated the same argument. In a speech before the James Madison Institute, Cheney affirmed, Saddam Hussein "had

---

[10] Ibid.
[11] Ibid.
[12] "Transcript of Interview with Vice President Dick Cheney," *Rocky Mountain News*, January 9, 2004.

long established ties with Al Qaeda."[13] Just two days later the independent commission investigating the September 11 attacks concluded that there was "no credible evidence" that Saddam Hussein had cooperated with Al Qaeda attacks against the United States.[14] Incredibly President Bush tried to defend his administration's position as being consistent with the commission's conclusion. "The reason I keep insisting that there was a relationship between Iraq and Saddam and Al Qaeda is because there was a relationship between Iraq and Al Qaeda but my administration never said that the 9/11 attacks were orchestrated between Saddam Hussein and Al Qaeda."[15] Bush's latter affirmation clearly contradicts statements that had been previously made by top administration officials.

Followers of Jesus Christ must have a high commitment to the truth. That commitment means more than just refraining from communicating falsehoods. It also means correcting falsehoods, even when that action is not convenient to your cause. The fact that key members of the Bush administration perpetuated the alleged, but false, connection between Saddam Hussein and the terrorist attacks of September 11 orchestrated by Al Qaeda and that they voluntarily communicated nothing to correct that misunderstanding by 70% of the United States population reveals a serious lack of integrity in our highest government officials.

---

[13] "Cheney Claims Ties between Saddam, Al Qaeda" http://www.cnn.com/2004/US/South/06/14/cheney.terrorism.ap/index.html.

[14] "Panel: No Iraq link to 9/11" in the *Chicago Tribune*, June 17, 2004, p. 1.

[15] "Bush insists that Iraq, al Qaeda had 'relationship'" June 17, 2004, http://www.cnn.com/2004/ALLPOLITICS/06/17/Bush.alqaeda/index.html.

II. The second allegation utilized by the Bush administration was that Saddam Hussein possessed weapons of mass destruction and would use them against the United States and the civilized world. This claim was repeated over and over again both to the North American public and to the larger international community. Democratic leaders such as Joseph Lieberman and Hillary Clinton voiced this same allegation. It was the principal argument that Colin Powell urged before the United Nations in his attempt to gain Security Council approval for military action against Iraq.

President Bush repeatedly affirmed that Iraq was an imminent danger to our country. His critics claim that he played upon the fear of the U.S. people. For example on October 7, 2002, he stated

> The danger to our country is grave. The danger to our country is growing. *The Iraqi regime possesses biological and chemical weapons.* The Iraqi regime is building the facilities necessary to make more biological and chemical weapons. And according to the British government the Iraqi regime could launch a biological or chemical attack in as little as 45 minutes after the order were given.... The regime is seeking *a nuclear bomb* and with fisible (sic), fissile material could build one within a year.... Facing clear evidence of peril, *we cannot wait for the final proof—the smoking gun—that could come in the form of a mushroom cloud.* [16]

President Bush argued his case in his State of the Union address on January 28, 2003. He affirmed, "Saddam Hussein had the materials to produce as much as 500 tons of sarin,

---

[16] *Uncovered: The Whole Truth about the Iraq War*, 2003.

mustard and VX nerve agent... Saddam Hussein had material sufficient to produce more than 38,000 liters of botulinum toxin, enough to subject millions of people to death by respiratory failure... the British government has learned that Saddam Hussein recently sought significant quantities of uranium from Africa."[17] The claim that, between 1999 and 2001, Iraq had purchased 500 tons of uranium oxide from Niger was in fact fallacious and based upon false documents. George Tenet, the Director of the Central Intelligence Agency, had already protested that claim and had overseen the removal of that accusation from a similar speech the president had given in Cincinnati on October 7, 2002.

Secretary of State Colin Powell repeated these claims when he went before the United Nations on February 5, 2003. He argued, *"Leaving Saddam Hussein in possession of weapons of mass destruction for a few more months or years is not an option... our conservative estimate is that Iraq today has a stockpile of between 100 and 500 tons of chemical weapons agent."*

Vice President Cheney affirmed on March 16, 2003, on the eve of the war, that the strongest reason for going to war was that "we believe *[Saddam Hussein] has,* in fact, *reconstituted nuclear weapons."*[18] His affirmation contradicted all the evidence. Just two weeks earlier the International Atomic Energy Agency had reported, *"There was no indication of resumed nuclear activities."*[19] Six months later, after the war had already been "justified" and executed, Cheney was

---

[17] President Bush's State of the Union Address, January 28, 2003.

[18] *Meet the Press*, NBC, March 16, 2003.

[19] *The Status of Nuclear Inspections in Iraq: An Update*, March 7, 2003.

questioned on the *Meet the Press* television program about his statement affirming that Saddam Hussein had possessed nuclear weapons on the eve of the war. He simply replied, *"I misspoke."*[20]

If there were doubts about Saddam Hussein's possession of weapons of mass destruction, surely after the coalition troops took control of Iraq the truth would come to the surface. High officials of the Bush administration had repeatedly affirmed that they knew where the weapons were. Powell had shown the United Nations pictures of the buildings and mobile units where weapon production was supposedly taking place.

Donald Rumsfeld constantly repeated that he knew where the weapons were located. Just two weeks into the war he affirmed, "We know where they are. They are in the area around Tikrit and Baghdad and east, west, south and north somewhat."[21] As months went by, no weapons of mass destruction were found. After two months, an administration spokesperson argued that more time was needed. "Come back in six months, if we haven't found the weapons by then, there will be a credibility problem." Six months came and went. No weapons of mass destruction were found. More than a year later, there is still a serious credibility problem.

The most conclusive and damning evidence comes not from Democrat critics but from within the Republican sphere of influence. In June 2003 the Bush administration appointed Dr. David Kay to head up the 1,200-member Iraq Survey Group to hunt for the weapons of mass destruction. After months of

---

[20] *Meet the Press*, NBC, September 14, 2003.
[21] *This Week with George Stephanopolous*, ABC, March 30, 2003.

fruitless investigation and $300 million of expenses, Dr. Kay resigned and admitted that United Nations inspections and Iraq's own destruction of their weapons had left Iraq with no stockpiles of chemical or biological weapons.[22] The evidence reveals that the affirmations about the weapons of mass destruction were completely false. Did the intelligence community mislead the President or did he mislead the Congress and the United States public? Republican John Dean, former White House Counsel to President Nixon in the early 1970s, commented on President Bush's 2003 State of the Union address and specifically on his affirmations regarding the weapons of mass destruction: "Bush presented so many distorted beliefs, estimates and guesstimates that *it appears he was misleading the public and the Congress....* The most troubling thing about the fact, the distortions and the misleading statements that Bush gave Congress is that it is *a federal felony, it's a crime, to mislead and distort information to present to the Congress.*"[23] This serious accusation by a respected member of the Republican establishment is further corroborated by a classified September 2002 report issued by the Pentagon's intelligence agency in which it warned that there was "no reliable information on whether Iraq is producing and stockpiling chemical weapons."[24]

---

[22] Richard W. Stevenson, "Iraq Illicit Arms Gone before War, Departing Inspector States", *New York Times*, January 24, 2004.

[23] *Uncovered: The Whole Truth about the Iraq War*, 2003.

[24] Defense Agency Issues Excerpt on Iraqi Chemical Warfare Program, State Department, June 7, 2003, http://usinfo.state.gov/topical/pol/arms/03060720.htm.

Whether President Bush himself was misled, whether he was just careless and foolhardy, or whether he deliberately misled others, the fact of the matter is that the allegation that Saddam Hussein had great amounts of weapons of mass destruction on the eve of the war has not been verified. No weapons of mass destruction have been found. In the past year many Iraqi scientists have been interrogated, and they all confirm that there were no such weapons.[25] At this point in the argument the alleged sincerity of President Bush is of no importance. The degree or lack of sincerity does not change the facts of the matter. In spite of the doubts coming from the United Nations Inspection Committee and even from the United States intelligence community itself regarding the existence of Iraqi weapons of mass destruction, the United States went to war based upon their supposed existence. The criterion for a just war was not fulfilled by this mistaken assumption.[26]

---

[25] Six months after Saddam Hussein's capture, many higher level officials in the Bush administration continue to affirm that such weapons of mass destruction did exist at the time of the war, but have now been lost, stolen or hidden. If this belief is true, it is even more troubling, because the alleged purpose of the war (i.e. to eliminate the WMD) has not been realized. If these weapons did exist, they are now probably in the hands of terrorists. These affirmations belie a desperate attempt to cover the tactics that they know were dishonest.

[26] Even staunch U.S. allies have felt betrayed by what they now perceive as a weapons of mass destruction pretext. Polish President Aleksander Kwasniewski, having sent 2400 troops to Iraq, confessed, "I feel uncomfortable [about Iraq] due to the fact that we were misled with the information on weapons of mass destruction." "Poland 'Misled' on Iraq, President Says", Associated Press, March 18, 2004.

III. The third argument is that Saddam Hussein was an evil tyrant who had committed genocide against his own people. On the surface, this claim is the strongest and seems to fit the just cause criterion. Saddam caused the killing of thousands of his Iraqi citizens. He used chemical weapons against Iran. In 1991 he invaded Kuwait. President Bush claimed, "This is a regime that has already used poison gas to murder thousands of its own citizens—leaving the bodies of mothers huddled over their dead children."[27] President Bush was correct in his denunciation of Saddam Hussein's atrocities.

Nevertheless, these accusations are seen by many Latin American Christians as *hypocrisy*. Many of the accusations of tyranny, abuse, and genocide refer to events that took place during the 1980s. In that period, the United States was supporting Saddam Hussein and Iraq in their war against Iran. The United States government, of which George Bush, Sr. was Vice President (1981-89) and President (1989-1993) respectively, knew about the "almost daily" use of chemical weapons by the Saddam Hussein regime. First, the United Nations criticized the Iraqi use of chemical weapons. Then on March 5, 1984, the Reagan administration itself issued a public condemnation of Iraq. In spite of those atrocities, the United States continued its support of Saddam Hussein. "The U. S. restored formal relations with Iraq in November 1984, but the U.S. had begun, several years earlier, to provide it with intelligence and military support (in secret and contrary to this

---

[27] President Bush's State of the Union Address, January 2002. Although it is true that Saddam Hussein brutally abused the Kurds, there is a continual debate whether the chemical weapons utilized against the Kurds came from Saddam or from the Iranians.

country's official neutrality) in accordance with policy directives from President Ronald Reagan."[28] Shortly after the U. S. condemnation of Iraqi chemical weapons, Donald Rumsfeld himself was sent as a special envoy of the Reagan administration to improve ties with "President Saddam Hussein."[29] Tariq Aziz, Iraq's foreign minister, commented that Saddam Hussein "was extremely pleased with Ambassador Rumsfeld's visit."[30] The Reagan administration provided Iraq with combat planning assistance. Our "highly classified program involved more than 60 officers of the Defense Intelligence Agency who shared intelligence on Iranian deployments, bomb-damage assessments and other crucial information with Iraq."[31] Tom Blanton, executive director of the National Security Archive, made this sad (from an ethical perspective) commentary: *"Saddam had chemical weapons in the 1980s, and it didn't make any difference to U. S. policy.... The embrace of Saddam in the 1980s and what it emboldened him to do should caution us as Americans that we have to look closely at all our murky alliances.... Shaking hands with dictators today can turn them into Saddams tomorrow."*[32]

It is generally admitted that Saddam Hussein was an evil tyrant that ruled over his own people mercilessly. Nevertheless,

---

[28] http://www.gwu.edu/~nsarchiv/NSAEBB/NSAEBB82/.

[29] The picture that is circulating widely these days of Donald Rumsfield shaking hands with Saddam Hussein comes from a meeting that took place in Baghdad on December 20, 1983. See http://www.gwu.edu/~nsarchiv/NSAEBB/NSAEBB82/ for greater details.

[30] Christopher Marquis, "Rumsfeld made Iraq Overture in '84 despite Chemical Raids" in the *New York Times*, December 23, 2003.

[31] Ibid.

[32] Ibid.

there are many other dictators in our world today, some having records even worse than Saddam Hussein's. Why did the Bush administration decide to wage war against Hussein and not against other evil tyrants? That question naturally leads into the second criterion, just intention.

Just Intention

This is one of the weakest links in the chain trying to justify the war in Iraq. As Holmes has clarified, "neither revenge nor conquest nor economic gain nor ideological supremacy are justified." Self-defense or defense of innocent victims would have been the most justified intention. Given that the "imminent danger of weapons of mass destruction" resolution before the United Nations was not accepted, a definite change occurred in the argumentation by the Bush administration. As the bombs began to fall, the war was dubbed "Operation Iraqi Freedom," thus pointing to a change in the attempts to justify it. The "just intention" became the "freedom of the Iraqi people" who were suffering intensely under the tyrannical Saddam Hussein. A nagging question still remained: Why Saddam and not other tyrants? Over the past decades there have been more violent, oppressive tyrants around the world. Neither George Bush, Sr. nor Bill Clinton nor George W. Bush did anything to remove the oppressors. In fact, during the presidential election campaign of 2000, George W. Bush disparaged the idea of "intervention and nation building" in other countries. He promised that under his administration the United States would be "humbler."

By definition, "intentions" are problematical to identify with exact precision. It is difficult to examine our own hearts and intentions, much less the intentions of another. But we must not shy away from this task. As we have seen in the preceding chapter, before the war started, our Latin American sisters and brothers suggested that some of the intentions of the Bush administration were not justified. They claimed that the Bush administration was more interested in Iraqi oil or regional hegemony than in the freedom of the Iraqi people. Evidence that has surfaced this past year demonstrates that our Latin American brethren were right. The overthrow of Saddam Hussein had been proposed by very influential members of the Bush administration long before the tragic events of September 11, 2001. The self-described "neo-conservatives" (Dick Cheney, Donald Rumsfeld, Paul Wolfowitz, etc.) had begun making the case for an American invasion of Iraq back in 1997.[33] They admitted that the removal of the dictator would be necessary for the United States to have access to inexpensive oil. It was suggested that the replacement of Saddam Hussein with a "puppet president" sympathetic to the United States might even lead to the downfall of OPEC. The protection of innocent Iraqis was not a part of this argument.

Deputy Defense Secretary Paul Wolfowitz has been the most outspoken member of the administration arguing for the removal of Saddam Hussein as the lynchpin for U.S. hegemony in the region. His removal would "convince" other Arab leaders to "fall into line." This goal of "ideological supremacy" is not acceptable according to Holmes' description of this Just War criterion.

As René Padilla demonstrates in the following chapter, U.S. military interventions on behalf of the "freedom" of other

---

[33] *Philly Daily News*, January 27, 2003.

countries have not always originated from "good intentions." Latin America has suffered so many interventions that it rightfully questions the validity of this often abused argument. The war in Iraq confirms their suspicions. Cheney said soldiers would be hailed as "liberators." Just two weeks before the invasion Paul Wolfowitz likened the invasion to World War II and affirmed, "Like the people of France in the 1940s, [the Iraqi people] view us as their hoped-for liberators." In fact, those predictions and celebrations were short-lived. Although most Iraqis probably were happy to see Saddam removed, the continuing attacks upon coalition soldiers demonstrate that many Iraqis view the United States as an undesirable occupation army. Even the Iraqi Governing Council (appointed by the United States) wanted to speed up the schedule and democratization for the turnover of power. Their demand for free and direct elections was not welcomed by the United States. The Bush administration first argued for a slower, more controllable caucus process. As the occupation has become more costly and more of a political liability, the U.S. government became more open to a quicker transferal of authority.

The teaching in the Bible urges Christians at least to consider the possibility of economic gain as a significant, albeit frequently hidden, motivation for wars. The Apostle James is quite clear when he asks the rhetorical question, "Where do wars come from?" He himself answers that the lust for possessions and the desire to gratify one's own pleasures motivate wars.[34] The Apostle Paul concurs when he affirms,

---

[34] James 4:1-3.

"The love of money is the root of all evil."[35] The evidence shows that economic factors were a very significant aspect of the war. After the major military fighting had been declared over, expensive contracts were granted, without bids, to certain favored companies. The most notorious case is the $7 billion contract granted to a Halliburton subsidiary, Kellogg, Brown & Root, in order to put out oil fires, import fuel and operate oil facilities in Iraq. This no-bid contract had been given to Halliburton even though the subsidiary had been found guilty of overcharging the United States Government by millions of dollars.[36] The conflict of interests implicated with Vice President Cheney's previous employer could not be more obvious.[37]

---

[35] I Timothy 6:10.

[36] In 2002 Brown & Root had paid $2 million to settle a criminal charge for overbilling the government. Letter from Rep. Henry Waxman and Rep. John Dingell to OMB Director Joshua Bolton, October 15, 2003. The overcharging continued in Iraq. "Jeffrey Jones, the Director of the Defense Energy Support Center (DESC), told minority staff of the House Government Reform Committee that it costs the DESC $1.08 to $1.19 to buy and import fuel via truck into Iraq—a price that's less than half the $2.65 Halliburton is charging the US government." Letter from Rep. Henry Waxman and Rep. John Dingell to Lt. Gen. Robert B. Flowers, U.S. Army Corps of Engineers, November 5, 2003. At White House insistence, the $87 billion emergency funding request had a measure removed that would have punished those who deliberately defrauded the United States with up to 20 years of prison.

[37] Vice President Dick Cheney had been the CEO of Halliburton up until 2000. On Sept. 14, 2003 Cheney affirmed on the NBC News program "Meet the Press" that "Since I left Halliburton to become George Bush's vice president, I've severed all my ties with the company, gotten rid of all my financial interest. I have no financial interest in Halliburton of any kind and haven't had, now, for over three years." Nevertheless, the Congressional Research Service ruled that Cheney did indeed have "a

In addition, the economic benefits promised as rewards of this war have not yet materialized, and the costs of the war were either grossly underestimated or deliberately misleading. The United States public was told that spending on Iraq would not be high because Iraqi oil production would essentially pay for the proposed war and for the later reconstruction.[38] That prediction was either a gross underestimate or a deliberate falsification. When White House economic adviser Lawrence Lindsey estimated that the Iraq intervention could cost up to $200 billion, he was summarily fired for his "whistle blowing"

---

continuing financial interest" in Halliburton as demonstrated by his 2001 deferred salary of $205,298, his 2002 salary of $162,392, and his 433,333 shares of stock in the company. "Cheney may still have Halliburton ties." http://money.cnn.com/2003/09/25/news/companies/cheney/?cnn=yes.

[38] In March, as the war began, Deputy Defense Secretary Paul Wolfowitz claimed revenues of $50-$100 billion from Iraqi oil could be expected within two to three years, declaring, "To assume that we're going to pay for it is just wrong.... We are dealing with a country that can really finance its own reconstruction, and relatively soon." "Rebuilding Costs to Be Shared; Rumsfeld tells Congress that taxpayers will get help from oil revenue, international donations," *LA Times*, March 28, 2003, p. 12. This rosy prediction was in direct contrast with the explanation given by George W. Bush's father for why he had not pursued the elimination of Saddam Hussein at the end of the Gulf War in 1991. "Trying to eliminate Saddam... would have incurred incalculable human and political costs.... We would have been forced to occupy Baghdad and, in effect, rule Iraq.... There was no viable 'exit strategy' we could see, violating another of our principles.... Going in and occupying Iraq, thus unilaterally exceeding the United Nations' mandate, would have destroyed the precedent of international response to aggression that we hoped to establish. Had we gone the invasion route, the United States could conceivably still be an occupying power in a bitterly hostile land. It would have been a dramatically different—and perhaps barren—outcome." George Bush and Brent Scowcroft, *A World Transformed*. New York: Knopf, 1998, p. 489.

candor. On October 4, 2002, Glen Hubbard, the President's top economist, claimed that "costs of any such intervention would be very small."[39] Four months later, Deputy Defense Secretary Paul Wolfowitz "dismissed articles in several newspapers that put the cost of war and reconstruction at $60 billion to $95 billion" for their excessive exaggeration of the figures.[40] On April 23, 2003, President Bush's top reconstruction official at the State Department told *Nightline* that "The American part of [reconstruction] will be $1.7 billion and we have no plans for further-on funding for this."[41] Just six weeks after announcing that "we don't anticipate requesting anything additional for the balance of this year," on September 7, 2003, President Bush asked Congress for an additional $87 billion, pushing the total cost to *$166 billion.*[42] According to the non-partisan Center for Strategic and Budgetary Assessments, the President would have to request another $50 billion, but for political reasons would delay it until after the November 2, 2004, presidential elections. That postponement was not feasible. On May 5, 2004, President Bush was forced to propose to Congress a request for another $25 billion to cover military operations, thus upping the total cost to *$191 billion.*[43]

The intentions suggested for going to war have been found to be deficient. Self-defense was not valid because Saddam

---

[39] CNBC, October 4, 2002.

[40] "Pentagon Contradicts General on Iraq Occupation Force's Size," *New York Times*, February 28, 2003.

[41] "Assistance for Iraq," *Nightline*, April 23, 2003.

[42] Presidential Address, September 7, 2003.

[43] "$25b sought for Iraq, Afghanistan," *The Boston Globe*, May 6, 2004.

Hussein did not collaborate in the 9/11 attacks. Protecting the world from Iraq's weapons of mass destruction might have been the sincere intent of the Bush administration, but the absence of WMD makes this goal suspect. The intention to make Iraq into a democracy and thus lead to a new era of United States hegemony and political stability in the Middle East was overly optimistic and lacked a sufficiently solid understanding of Arab religion and culture. Perhaps the desire for cheap oil was not the primary intention for going to war. Nevertheless, the fact that estimated revenues from oil production were definitely considered in the anticipated costs of the war leads to the conclusion that this intention did play a role in the war plans and was not justified.

Last Resort

On various occasions President Bush recognized the validity of the "Last Resort" criterion and claimed that it had been more than fulfilled. He repeatedly stated his position, *"I'm reluctant to use military power. It's the last choice; it's not our first choice."*[44] On the eve of the invasion the President affirmed, "The American people can know that every measure has been taken to avoid war."[45] Many citizens of the United States believe that our country is the "reluctant warrior" who only goes into battle after all other options have been exhausted.

---

[44] Presidential Press Conference, December 16, 2003.
[45] Presidential Speech, March 17, 2003.

Towards the end of 2002 and during the first months of 2003 President Bush claimed that he was still seeking a diplomatic solution and wanted to avoid war: "I hope this will not require military action."[46] Nevertheless, other evidence suggests that the administration had already decided to go to war against Iraq even as it continued to talk about peace. In fact, the invasion of Iraq had been suggested by the Neo-Conservatives years before, and they were just waiting for a pretext to implement their plan. The attacks on September 11, 2001, became the perfect motive. The very next day in the situation room of the White House, Rumsfeld asked the question, *"Shouldn't we use this as an opportunity to do something about Iraq as well?"*[47] This question of doing "something about Iraq" was raised even though Vice President Dick Cheney admitted five days later that there was no evidence of Iraq's involvement in the terrorist attacks of September 11,[48] a position he soon altered, as we have discussed. Within the administration there were disagreements on strategy, but waging war on Saddam was never really in doubt. Deputy Defense Secretary Paul Wolfowitz stated that, despite having no immediate reason for overthrowing Saddam, "the disagreement [in the weekend after 9/11/01] was whether [invading Iraq] should be in the immediate response or whether you should concentrate simply on Afghanistan first."[49] In March of 2002 President Bush told a

---

[46] Presidential Speech, October 7, 2002.

[47] Bill Christison in *Uncovered: The Whole Truth about the Iraq War*, 2003.

[48] *"Meet the Press"* NBC, September 16, 2001.

[49] Deputy Secretary Wolfowitz Interview with Vanity Fair's Sam Tannenhaus, *DefenseLink*, May 9, 2003.

group of senators, *"f... [expletive] Saddam. We're taking him out."*[50] Vice President Cheney gave senators the same message, *"The question was no longer if the U.S. would attack Iraq.... The only question was when."*[51] The revelation of these declarations from the spring of 2002 makes later affirmations of a willingness to pursue diplomatic solutions sound very hypocritical indeed.

The world community urged Bush to walk the extra mile. After Secretary of State Powell made his argument before the United Nations, key members of the Security Council proposed a counter resolution asking for a few more weeks of investigation and negotiation. Bush refused to do so, even though he would have obtained the "super majority" vote required on the Security Council. The evidence suggests that the administration had already decided to go to war against Iraq even as it continued to talk about peace. Chief United Nations inspector in Iraq Hans Blix offered his opinion which is widely shared by the international community, "I still thought that three and a half months for new inspections was a rather short time...especially now that the U.S. government is now saying you have to have a bit of patience, you know these things take time."[52]

---

[50] "We're Taking Him Out", Time.com, May 5, 2002. This use of profanity by the President in an unguarded moment seems to reveal that the war was considered to be somewhat of a macho game rather than a reasoned, statesmanlike decision of last resort.

[51] Ibid.

[52] *Uncovered: The Whole Truth about the Iraq War*, 2003.

Formal Declaration

This rule states that because the use of military force is the prerogative of governments, not of private individuals, a state of war must be officially declared by the highest authorities. This criterion has been understood as the prerogative of national governments or of international bodies. The formal declaration must be linked to the "just cause" that is articulated. If Saddam Hussein had been involved in the 9/11 attacks, then the United States Government through its Congress would have been the appropriate body to declare war upon Iraq. That was not the case.

The events leading up to the war in Iraq demonstrate that the United Nations was the most appropriate authority to declare war. The United Nations exercised the sanctions against Iraq after the first Gulf War. These included the limits on exportation of oil for food as well as limits on arms.

The Bush administration recognized, in theory, the authority of the United Nations. On September 12, 2002, President Bush himself addressed the United Nations General Assembly. He then sent Secretary of State Colin Powell to address the UN in an attempt to persuade the Security Council to declare war. Then the Bush proposal was drafted and circulated among the Security Council members by Spain and England. For the proposal to be accepted, nine of the fifteen members, the so-called "Super Majority," needed to approve it. Early on, it was clear that the United States, Great Britain, Spain, and Bulgaria would vote in favor of the proposal. It was also clear that Russia, France, and China would vote against it. That left the decision in the hands of the swing members. The two Latin American member states, Chile and Mexico, opposed the resolution. Much pressure, totally unrelated to the merits of the proposed war on Iraq, was applied to these countries in an attempt to persuade them. For example, Mexico's President Fox was promised changes on immigration laws for Mexicans entering the United States. The Bush administration threatened that the free trade agreement with Chile would be in danger unless Chile voted in favor the resolution. Chile opposed the war resolution and the trade agreement was, in fact, postponed.

In spite of the arguments put forth by Powell and in spite of the "strong arm" tactics that the United States pursued to obtain the necessary nine votes on the Security Council, the United States was not able to obtain the United Nations' authorization. Unable to garner the necessary votes, the United States withdrew its proposal and launched its own military attack. *It is precisely at this point that the war on Iraq clearly did not meet the formal declaration criterion for a just war, because the United Nations did not approve the resolution.*

It is here that Just War Christians must be honest with their own principles if they are to be taken seriously. In his justification of the 1991 Persian Gulf War, George Weigel affirmed that the 1991 Gulf War did meet this criterion precisely because the United Nations had authorized it.[53] The

---

[53] George Weigel, "From Last Resort to Endgame: Morality, the Gulf War, and the Peace Process" in David E. Decosse, ed. *But Was It Just? Reflections on the Morality of the Persian Gulf War.* New York: Doubleday, 1992, p. 22. Regarding the 1991 Persian Gulf War Weigel claimed that "the use of armed force by the coalition led by the United States was authorized by a resolution of the Security Council of the United Nations.

2003 war in Iraq did not meet this criterion. Given that the resolution proposed before the United Nations argued that Saddam Hussein possessed (and would use) weapons of massive destruction and given the fact that no such weapons have been found more than one year after the invasion, it must be concluded that *the United Nations was morally right to reject the resolution.*[54]

At a lower level, the "formal declaration" rule was treated within the United States Government. According to the United States Constitution, *only* Congress has the power to declare war on a foreign country. Nevertheless, President Bush wanted sweeping powers to be given to the executive branch. As a result, the White House sent a "discussion draft" resolution to Capitol Hill in September 2002. It was really a "blank check" to do whatever was necessary in Iraq and in the "region." Whereas Bush was seeking a more limited objective from the United Nations (the elimination of Iraqi weapons of mass destruction), he desired more ambitious powers (total regime change in Iraq) from the United States Congress. Republicans and Democrats alike did not fulfill their constitutional

---

At every significant decision point between August 2, 1990, and February 28, 1991, the United States engaged in extensive consultations with its principal allies, including major Arab states. In short, the Gulf War was authorized, not just once, but in a continuing process of international agreement, by all the relevant 'competent authorities'."

[54] It is here that I am personally saddened by the actions of many of my fellow Christians. Instead of ridiculing the French and others for their "lack of backbone," Christians who supported the war for the wrong reasons should admit that they were misled by their own government. Consequently, they should ask the tough questions of their government leaders rather than sweeping the dirt under the rug.

responsibilities because they transferred to the President these extraordinary powers.

Veteran West Virginia Democrat Senator Robert Byrd, an expert on congressional legal issues, was one of the lonely, prophetic voices that questioned this procedure. He lamented:

> Our Senate was, for the most part, silent—dreadfully silent. There is no debate, no discussion, no attempt to lay out for the nation the pros and cons of this particular war. There is nothing. This nation is about to embark on the first test of a revolutionary doctrine applied in an extraordinary way at an unfortunate time. *The doctrine of pre-emption—the idea that the United States or any other nation can legitimately attack a nation that is not imminently threatening but may be threatening in the future—is a radical new twist on the traditional idea of self-defense.* In pursuit of this doctrine, the administration has split traditional alliances, possibly crippling for all time international order-keeping entities like the United Nations and NATO. This administration has called into question the traditional worldwide perception of the United States as well-intentioned peacekeeper. This administration has turned the patient art of diplomacy into threats, labeling and name-calling.... Calling heads of state "pygmies," labeling whole countries as evil, denigrating powerful European allies as irrelevant—these types of insensitivities can do our great nation no good. Yet, this chamber is hauntingly silent.... We are truly "sleepwalking through history."[55]

---

[55] Doug Cassel, "The Irresponsible Nation: U.S. has blown up rule of law and order," *The Chicago Tribune*, March 23, 2003. Cassel's opinion is important because he is the Director of the Center for International Human Rights at Northwestern University's School of Law and because

Senator Byrd rightfully points out that not only did the administration fail to meet the criterion of formal declaration, but it also weakened the authority, and therefore the ability, of the United Nations to mediate in other locations in the future.

There were other prophetic voices that rose up to challenge this maneuver. Ray McGovern, a CIA analyst with 27 years of experience, rightfully unmasks the deception that was utilized: "Weapons of mass destruction was a convenient way of tricking our Congress into giving the President authority to wage this war."[56]

Limited Objectives

According to Holmes, the criterion of limited objectives means that "if the purpose is peace, then unconditional surrender or the destruction of a nation's economic or political institutions is an unwarranted objective."[57] Therefore, it is questionable whether the war in Iraq met this condition. If the objective was to eliminate Saddam Hussein's weapons of mass destruction, then that had apparently taken place years before the war broke out. Saddam's cat-and-mouse games with the United Nations inspectors might reveal his own macho bravado or a tactical bluff. Nevertheless, the fact that Hans Blix and his inspectors had not found weapons in more than three months of fairly unrestricted searches did not justify an

---

Christian convictions underlie his arguments.

[56] *Uncovered: The Whole Truth about the Iraq War*, 2003.

[57] Holmes, "The Just War," p. 121.

invasion of Iraq. The Security Council acted correctly in rejecting the resolution.

Regime change, by itself, is not a valid objective. Was regime change necessary to achieve *freedom* and *democracy* for the Iraqi people? Possibly. Was the destruction of Iraq's economic and political institutions (i.e., the Iraqi police force) warranted? No. Even the Bush administration has admitted this mistake. The destruction of the Iraqi police force led to greater looting, unrest, and violence, transforming the reconstruction process into a prolonged, costly and violent occupation. Billions of dollars are being invested in the reconstruction of Iraq's infrastructure. To his credit, Bush pressured his own Republican congressional representatives not to make this "assistance" to Iraq in the form of a loan that would need to be repaid. Nevertheless, attempts to rebuild Iraq's schools, police force, health and educational services, etc., have been met with substantial opposition by Iraqis who perceive the coalition not as liberators but as foreign occupation forces. Because the administration underestimated the breadth of Iraqi opposition to their attempts at reconstruction, it is still questionable whether the objectives of freedom and democracy will be realized.

Proportionate Means

Whether the war in Iraq fulfilled this criterion is debatable. In Holmes' terms "the weaponry and the force used should be limited to what is needed to repel the aggression and deter future attacks, that is to say, to secure a just peace. Total or unlimited war is ruled out."[58] Were the indiscriminant "shock and awe" bombings excessive? Yes. On the other hand, did the coalition soldiers demonstrate restraint in their military actions? On many occasions, yes, they did. Stories abound of the numerous kind acts performed by coalition soldiers on behalf of Iraqis.

One of the most questionable practices has to do with the treatment of prisoners. In May 2004 pictures leaked out to the press of the abuses that took place in the Abu Ghraib prison. Torture, sexual humiliation, sleep deprivation and vicious dogs were part of the treatment used against Iraqi prisoners of war in order to gain information from them. Debate rages on how widespread these abuses were. The administration claims that those who performed these actions were just "a few bad apples." The administration's critics believe that the abuses were more widespread. The soldiers who have been accused of these abuses claim that they were acting upon orders from their superiors. Although at the time of writing the final findings have not yet come out there are some troublesome signs at a wider level. The administration did not extend the Geneva Conventions rights of prisoners of war to those in prison at Guantanamo Bay, Cuba, by classifying them as "enemy combatants."[59] There are indications that the prisoners in the

---

[58] Ibid.

[59] Although it is well known that suspected jihadists are detained in the Guantanamo prison, it is not so widely known that the United States operates a half-dozen others in Jordan, Afghanistan, and on the island of Diego Garcia in the Indian Ocean. Even allied governments, such as Indonesia, have been refused access to their own citizens in these prisons. "Inside the Iraq Prison Scandal" *U.S. News &World Report*, May 24, 2004, p. 27.

Iraqi prisons, including those at Abu Ghraib, were also not completely protected by the Geneva Conventions, especially after Major General Geoffrey Miller, in command of the detention facility in Guantanamo, visited the Iraqi prisons in August, 2003, and made recommendations to obtain information. Some of the harshest criticism has arisen from the Republican ranks. "Over time, we will find that this was not just rogue MP behavior," affirmed Senator Lindsey Graham, Republican on the Armed Services Committee. "How could we let this prison melt down and become the worst excuse for a military organization I've seen in my life?"[60]

An unclassified 2002 Justice Department memorandum describing legal justifications for torture was sent to the White House.[61] Additional memoranda written by lawyers within the Defense Department and other agencies argued that "inflicting pain in interrogating people detained in the fight against terrorism did not always constitute torture" and that "President Bush was not bound by either an international treaty prohibiting torture or by a federal anti-torture law."[62]

On this issue of abuse, the conservative evangelical magazine *Christianity Today* took a clear stand. Based upon the theologies of Augustine and Luther, Steven Gertz wrote that American soldiers "at Abu Ghraib failed on at least two accounts—working counter to the purpose of peace, and if some reports are true, failing to disobey orders that no

---

[60] Ibid.

[61] http://www.washingtonpost.com/wp-dyn/articles/A24867-2004 Jun8.html

[62] Neil A. Lewis, "Bush Didn't Order any Breach of Torture Laws, Ashcroft Says" *The New York Times*, June 9, 2004.

Christian could in good conscience follow."[63] The article went on to affirm that Christians need to protest the abuse of power. It then praised the work of "the *Christian Peacemaker Teams'* presence in Iraq, calling commanders of military bases to account for injustice done to prisoners, attempting to help Iraqis gain access to family and friends imprisoned in Abu Ghraib, and urging police to cajole Army officers into acting on the abuses."[64] Gertz ended his article with an exhortation to Christians.

> Let's rightly react with revulsion when we see these pictures and call for an accounting for the crimes committed. But let's also recognize the evil nature in ourselves, and out of this recognition, cheer on the work of Christian Peacemaker Teams and others seeking to counter the evil done by Christians who have failed to live up to their calling. May God have mercy on us and the guards and the prisoners of Abu Ghraib.[65]

Noncombatant Immunity

Holmes explains this criterion as follows: "Since war is an official act of government, only those who are officially agents of government may fight, and individuals not actively contributing to the conflict (including POWs and casualties as well as civilian nonparticipants) should be immune from

---

[63] Steven Gertz, "I Was in Prison and You Abused Me: What would Jesus do at Abu Ghraib?" at http://www.chrisitanitytoday.com/ct/2004/121/53.0.html
[64] Ibid.
[65] Ibid.

attack." In the war in Iraq did civilians receive the immunity required? There is evidence on both sides of this debate.

On the one hand, much was made of the coalition's "smart bombs." A week and a half into the invasion, Rumsfeld boasted: "Our military capabilities are so devastating and precise that we can destroy an Iraqi tank under a bridge without damaging the bridge. We do not need to kill thousands of innocent Iraqis to remove Saddam Hussein from power."[66] These technological wonders could pinpoint their targets and thereby reduce the "collateral damage," that is, the deaths and injuries that were unintentional consequences of the bombs. Were these bombings a moral improvement on the indiscriminant air bombings of World War II? Yes. Did these smart bombs meet the criteria's standards? Probably not, because many of these "smart" bombs produced exploding shrapnel that did in fact kill innocent civilians. Other bombs were "mistakenly" dropped upon wedding parties or other cultural gatherings that had nothing to do with the opposition fighters. According to the organization *Iraq Body Count*, as of August 20, 2004, a minimum of 11,619 civilians (and perhaps up to 13,603 civilians) were killed in the military intervention in Iraq.[67]

Conclusion

The criteria of the Just War Theory, if applied faithfully, are high standards to meet... and rightfully so. If we are to

---

[66] Derrick A. Jackson, "Bush Speech Spins the Winds of War" in the *Chicago Tribune*, June 7, 2004, p.21.

[67] http://iraqbodycount.net/

suspend such commands in Scripture as "Thou shalt not kill," "Turn the other cheek," and "Love your enemies," we must have clear and powerful overriding arguments. Christians who believe in Just War Theory must be rigorous in the application of those criteria if they want to be taken seriously.

We believe that the war in Iraq failed to satisfy the criteria of a Just War and most grievously the first four criteria. Because all seven criteria must be fulfilled for a war to be considered "justified" we believe that this war failed to satisfy the necessary conditions. Sincere Christians might disagree with us on some of our evaluations. We welcome further discussion by our brothers and sisters in Christ as we together strive to walk more faithfully in the steps of the Prince of Peace.

3

United States Foreign Policy and Terrorism

The fruit of righteousness will be peace;
the effect of righteousness will be quietness and confidence forever.
(Isaiah 32:17)

I urge, then . . . that requests, prayers, intercession and thanksgiving
be made for everyone—for kings and all those in authority,
that we may live peaceful and quiet lives in all godliness and holiness.
(1 Timothy 2:1-2)

September 11, 2001, will be remembered in the United States and in many other countries as one of the darkest days of modern history. Surpassing every possible forecast, terrorism was able to convert three commercial jets with passengers on board into powerful bombs, two of which hit the Twin Towers in New York while the third one hit the Pentagon in Washington D. C. Intelligence placed at the service of the crudest kind of violence killed over two thousand people and plunged their families and friends into mourning. It was an execrable act of madness against the most important symbols of the economic and military power of the present-day empire—the United States. Anyone with a minimal sense of respect for human life cannot but repudiate that act of aggression, which has been described as "the most serious terrorist attack in history." The scene produced by the suicide attack proved once again that reality can in fact go beyond fiction. How can one abstain from lamenting the killing of so many people and all the suffering resulting from it?

What happened in New York and Washington D. C., however, calls for a careful reflection on the causes behind the horrible terrorist attack. Was it really an attack provoked by the United States' love for freedom, as President George W. Bush affirmed in his speech on the day it took place?

Quite frankly, I flatly reject that explanation. To be sure, I regard myself as a sincere admirer of the people of North American. Indeed, I am indebted to many individuals and institutions from the United States, and deeply grateful for all that they have meant to me and my family. Because of that, however, at this difficult time in their history I feel compelled to say that the United States as a nation is harvesting what it has sown. What is true of individuals is also true of nations—the one that sows death harvests death; the one that sows terror harvests terror.

Does that mean, then, that the United States has sown terror?

Over a decade ago, a distinguished U. S. Senator, J. William Fulbright, wrote a book dealing with the delicate question of U. S. foreign policy—*The Price of Empire*.[1] Having chaired the Senate Committee on International Relations for almost thirty years (from 1945 to 1974), and in cooperation with Seth T. Tillman, a Georgetown University professor expert in issues of international diplomacy, the illustrious Senator denounced what he called "the arrogance of power" which marks U. S. relations with other countries around the world. According to him, *the repeated acts of interventionism in the internal affairs of so-called third-world countries cannot be justified even if they are carried*

---

[1] New York: Pantheon Books, 1989.

out in the name of freedom and democracy. The real bottom line, according to Fulbright, *is U. S. economic interests.* In order to protect those interests, the U. S. government time after time has been willing to align "against those who would strike at corruption and tyranny, on the side of the traditional elite and militarists who have kept their people in line."[2] And sadly, the evidence to demonstrate that the superpower's use of violence to protect its economic interests includes terrorism is such that Fulbright categorically states: *"We and some of our friends have initiated some of the worst aspects of modern terrorism."*[3] My purpose in this chapter is to show that the history of U. S.-Latin American relations substantiates Fulbright's indictment and leads to the conclusion that the proper response to the terrorism perpetrated in New York on September 11, 2001, is not war waged in the name of freedom and democracy—U. S. terrorism—,[4] but a total reorientation of U. S. foreign policy in favor of world peace and justice.

---

[2] Ibid., p. 159.

[3] Ibid., p. 172, emphasis mine.

[4] The reference to the War in Iraq as "U. S. terrorism" presupposes a comprehensive definition of terrorism such as the one that Lee Griffiths adapts from a Quaker study: "Terrorism is a tactic, whether used by an established government, a revolutionary group, or an individual." Quoted by Robert Jewett & John Shelton Lawrence in *Captain America and the Crusade Against Evil: The Dilemma of Zealous Nationalism* (Grand Rapids: Wm. B. Eerdmans Publishing Co., 2003), p. 20. According to Noam Chomsky in *Pirates and Emperors, Old and New* (London: Pluto Press, 2002), the term "terrorism" was originally used in the eighteenth century to refer to violent acts carried out by governments for the purpose of keeping the people in subjection. That connotation, however, has been lost, and the term is mainly applied to violent acts committed by groups or individuals.

I. U. S.-Latin American Relations:
A Case Study of U. S. Foreign Policy

The history of relations between the United Sates and Latin America beginning in the nineteenth century provides ample support for Senator Fulbright's harsh indictment. There is no exaggeration in saying that *the hallmark of U. S. foreign policy has been and continues to be interference in the internal affairs of its southern neighbors for the sake of U. S. economic interests.* Behind the U. S. policy of intervention lies the assumption that there is an inter-American system ruled by the Monroe Doctrine, in which all the American countries share common interests. The historical study of U. S.-Latin American relations, however, shows that the Monroe Doctrine has been consistently used to advance U. S. political and economic interests as a world power.

The Monroe Doctrine

The revolution against Spain on the part of its colonies in Latin America beginning in 1810 posed a problem to the U. S. government. Both President Madison and President Monroe adopted a position of neutrality. This lack of support to Latin American independence was to some extent the result of an attitude which prevailed in the early stage of this relationship and was eloquently expressed by Secretary of State John Quincy Adams:

> I have not yet seen and do not now see any prospect that they will establish free or liberal institutions of government.... They have not the first elements of good or free government.... We shall derive no improvement to our own institutions by any communion with theirs. Nor is there any

appearance of a disposition in them to take any political lesson from us.[5]

On December 2, 1823, in his annual speech to the Congress, President Monroe articulated what is now regarded as the basic statement of inter-American relations: *The Monroe Doctrine*. The speech was provoked by a decree issued by Czar Alexander I of Russia, warning foreign vessels not to come within 100 miles of the coast of Alaska. In it President Monroe defined hemispheric relations in the Americas over against any attempt on the part of the colonial powers to reestablish their control over any of their former colonies. He warned that any such attempt would be considered as "dangerous to our peace and safety" and as "the manifestation of an unfriendly disposition toward the United States."[6] This was a declaration of the United States as the protector of the hemisphere, in charge of the security of all the new American nations. Its real intent was to safeguard U. S. western expansion without competition on the part of European nations. *Long before it had become a world power, the U. S. was assuming a hegemonic role in relation to the whole region*. Not until the 1850s would this declaration become known as *The Monroe Doctrine*. But it was the earliest official definition of a principle which would color the whole history of the relations between the United States and Latin America.

The Monroe Doctrine was a self-appointment; the Latin American countries were not consulted on the matter of their security over against the European powers. The U. S. govern-

---

[5] Quoted in Michael J. Kryzanek, *U. S.-Latin American Relations* (New York: Praeger Publishers, 2nd ed., 1990), p. 24.

[6] Quoted by Kryzanek, ibid., p. 25.

ment simply assumed that the Latin American countries would be either under its control or under the control of its enemies. Such an assumption has always been present in the relationship between the two Americas. In theory, the purpose of the Monroe Doctrine was to protect the Latin American republics from foreign intervention. In practice, from the beginning the true purpose proved to be to safeguard U. S. political and economic interests in the whole hemisphere and to extend U. S. dominion over the whole region. The annexation of Texas, New Mexico, California and Arizona to the U. S. in the 1840s and 1850s was the first concrete demonstration that the real threat to the national integrity of the Latin American countries would not come from Europe but from their northern neighbor.

The same message was conveyed again by the way in which the U. S. dealt with New Granada (now Colombia) to gain control over Panama in order to construct a canal across the isthmus. The 1848 Bidlack Treaty, through which the United States guaranteed "the rights of sovereignty and of property" that New Granada held over the isthmus of Panama, was "the only occasion in the nineteenth century in which the United States accepted the overture of a Latin American state to defend its sovereignty."[7] But the signing of the contract was only a way to discourage Great Britain from using its own colony on the eastern coast of Central America as a base from which to control the isthmus. Two years later, in 1850, the U. S. and Great Britain signed the Clayton-Bulwe Treaty, by which the two countries agreed to cooperate in the construction of a railway or a canal to link the two oceans and to maintain the isthmus as neutral territory. The intention of keeping European powers out of the

---

[7] Ibid., p. 30.

region was thus forgotten by the U. S. for the sake of reaching a diplomatic settlement with its most powerful competitor in Latin America.

The ineffectiveness of the Monroe Doctrine was again made evident in 1895, on occasion of a boundary dispute between Venezuela and British-held Guyana. In his message to London, Secretary of State Richard Olney demanded that the British submit the matter to international arbitration. To bolster his demand and echoing President Grover Cleveland, Olney declared:

> Today the United States is practically sovereign on the continent, and its fiat is law upon the subjects to which it confines its interposition. Why? ... because in addition to all other grounds, its infinite resources combined with its isolated position render it master of the situation and practically invulnerable as against any or all other posers.[8]

Pressed by more important concerns in South Africa and in Canada, the British agreed to submit the boundary dispute to arbitration. When the matter was finally settled in 1899, however, they retained most of what they had originally claimed.

From Monroe to Reagan: Interventionism and the Shaping of the Empire

The U. S. position as a world power was greatly strengthened by the results of the Spanish-American war in 1898. Anxious to protect its economic holdings (by the 1880s the U. S. had in

---

[8] Quoted by Kryzanek, *U. S.-Latin American Relations*, p. 33.

Cuba $50 million in investments and $100 million in trade),[9] Congress passed a resolution to force the withdrawal of Spain from the island and to secure its independence. Within three months the war was over and Spain was forced to make three concessions defined by the Treaty of Paris, signed on December 10, 1898, with no Cuban citizen present: (a) to recognize the independence of Cuba; (b) to cede Puerto Rico and the Pacific Island of Guam; (c) to sell the Philippine Islands for $20 million. By the same treaty, "the political rights and condition" of Cuba would be defined by the Congress of the United States.[10] This dominion over Cuba was consolidated by the so-called Platt Amendment, approved by Congress in March 1901, by which the U. S. claimed the right to control the Island economically and politically, in order "to maintain the independence of Cuba and to protect the people thereof, as well as for its own defense."[11] *Definitely, the United States had become an imperial power, quite disposed to control the destiny of its Latin American neighbors.*

With President Theodore Roosevelt, who ascended to national leadership in 1901, the politics of colonial expansion became firmly established. First, through negotiations with Great Britain, the Clayton-Bulwer agreement of 1850 was replaced by the Hay-Paunceforte Treaty that granted the U. S. the right to build, control, and fortify a future Panama canal. Then, in June of

---

[9] Ibid., p. 35.

[10] Cf. Gordon Connell-Smith, *United States and Latin America: An Historical Analysis of Inter-American Relations* (London: Heinemann Educational), p. 128.

[11] Quoted by Kryzanek, op. cit., p.37, from Article VII of the Platt Amendment.

1902, Roosevelt was authorized by the Senate to negotiate with Colombia for a way to build the canal in its province of Panama. Secretary of State John Hay succeeded in signing an agreement with the Colombian representative, Tomas Harran, by which Colombia agreed to lease to the U. S. a zone six miles wide on either side of the canal for the amount of $10 million and an annual payment of $250,000 beginning in ten years. The treaty, however, was rejected by the Colombian Senate, which regarded the compensation as insufficient. Displeased, Roosevelt found a way to speed up the negotiations with the help of the French representative of the canal company, Philippe Bunau-Varilla. With U. S. support, Bunau-Varilla organized a Panamenian revolution. On November 4, 1903, Panama declared its independence from Colombia; on November 6 President Roosevelt recognized the new nation, and on November 18 Hay and Bunau-Varilla, in representation of the U. S. and Panama respectively, signed a treaty by whose terms the U. S. paid the new government $10 million and $250,000 a year for a zone that had been widened from six to ten miles, leased "in perpetuity." The rational behind this action was clearly defined by President Roosevelt in a message to Congress on December 6, 1904:

> Chronic wrongdoing, or an impotence which results in a general loosening of the ties of civilized society, may in America, as elsewhere, ultimately require intervention by some civilized nation, and in the Western Hemisphere the adherence of the United States, however reluctantly…to the exercise of an international police power.[12]

---

[12] Theodore Roosevelt, quoted by Kryzanek, op. cit., p. 42.

Thus, with what came to be known as the *Roosevelt Corollary,* the Monroe Doctrine was transformed from a principle regarding defense against foreign intervention into a policy that assigned to the U. S. the task of intervening in order to establish *political and financial order* anywhere in the hemisphere. The *Big-Stick* Era, with its emphasis on *stability for the sake of social, economic, and political development,* had arrived. In retrospect, it may be said that this *Big-Stick* policy prepared the way for the policy of terror which became the order of the day during the so-called *Cold War* following the World War II.

Roosevelt's immediate successors William Howard Taft and Woodrow Wilson reedited the interventionist policy of their predecessor. The *Dollar Diplomacy* of the former and the *Civilizing Policy* of the latter were variations of a consistent approach through which U. S. economic and political interests were served particularly in Haiti, the Dominican Republic, Nicaragua and Cuba. The record of their interventions in the internal affairs of these countries left no doubt as to the extent to which *the basic issue for the U. S. in its relations with Latin America was the political stability of the region, if necessary through military means, as a condition for U. S. economic and strategic goals.* It consistently demonstrated that U. S. foreign policy in Latin America was a new form of colonialism.

The Good Neighbor Policy

During the Republican era, under Harding, Coolidge, and Hoover, efforts were made to steer foreign policy away from direct intervention by the removal of the military from the Caribbean and Central American protectorates. Nicaragua, for instance, which had been under U. S. military control almost uninterruptedly since 1912, bid farewell to the Marines in 1933, under President Hoover. The time had come to let the local constabularies do the job of maintaining order, for which they had been diligently trained by the U. S. administration. In the case of this Central American country, the task was committed to Anastasio Somoza, head of the Nicaraguan National Guard, who plotted the assassination of his populist adversary, Augusto Sandino, and started a ruthless dictatorship which lasted until 1979.

Hoover has sometimes been praised for doing more than anyone else to reverse the foreign policy of the "great interventionists" of the first decades of the twentieth century. He did seem in fact to be less inclined to take up the defense of private enterprises against Latin American governments. There is, however, evidence that under his administration Latin American economic dependence reached a peak, but he did nothing to limit exploitation. On the contrary, he contributed to worsening the situation by signing the *Hawley-Smoot Tariff Act* of 1930 and the *Revenue Act* of 1932, two achievements of U. S. protectionism.

With Franklin D. Roosevelt the *Good Neighbor* policy came into its own. In his inaugural presidential address on March 4, 1933, he promised to dedicate the nation to "the policy of the good neighbor—the neighbor who resolutely respects himself and, because he does, respects the rights of others—the neighbor who respects his obligations and respects the sanctity of his agreements in and with a world of neighbors."[13] In line with this intent, he promoted a number of significant changes in U. S.-Latin American relations. Perhaps the best illustration of this new

---

[13] Franklin D. Roosevelt quoted in Kryzanek, op. cit., p. 53.

approach to foreign policy was the way in which he acted when Mexican President Lázaro Cárdenas expropriated oil holdings owned by U. S. companies that had failed to comply with court decisions regarding the rights of workers. To the dismay of the affected companies, Roosevelt refused to interfere and chose to let the matter be settled by the World Court. Other evidences of the Good Neighbor policy were the abrogation of the Platt Amendment in 1934, which changed the political situation of Cuba, and the signing of a new treaty with Panama in 1936, recognizing it as an independent state.

World War II also modified the relations between the U. S. and their neighbors to the south during the Roosevelt era. Initially the Latin American republics refused to cooperate with the alliance against the Axis countries. Gradually, especially after Pearl Harbor, they received scores of U. S. military advisors, leased land to the U. S. for military bases, bought great quantities of U. S. weapons, and became producers and exporters of strategic materials such as tungsten, rubber, and tin. Thus, in the name of a neighborly spirit, *the needs of people in Latin America were made subservient to the demands of the new political and economic order that had emerged with the U. S. as its center.*

Between East and West

At the end of World War II the Latin American countries discovered how much they had become part of a world system dominated by two superpowers, the United States and the Soviet Union, each seeking to extend its own sphere of influence and to prevent the other from doing the same. Under both Truman and Eisenhower U. S. foreign policy began to have as its central concern the prevention of the advance of communism and the support of governments that would quell any and every revolutionary movement. To be sure, in the past Washington had already on occasions justified military intervention as a means to protect freedom and democracy against communist encroachments.[14] The same justification had been given for the friendly attitude of U. S. government officials toward Latin American dictators such as Trujillo in the Dominican Republic and Somoza in Nicaragua.[15] After World War II, however, the *Cold War* started and the strict ideological bipolarity between East and West focused U. S. foreign policy mainly on the containment of Soviet expansion. *Anti-communism became a rallying point for people with the most diverse interests,* and this broad consensus provided the basis for the creation of a military alliance among the nations of the hemisphere. The United States led them to sign the *Inter-American Treaty of Reciprocal Assistance* in Rio de Janeiro in 1947, but turned a deaf ear to a request which was voiced by them a year later at the inaugural meeting of the Organization of American States (OAS) in Bogota: the request for assistance akin to the Marshall Plan in Europe, for economic reconstruction. Quite clearly, *the urgent needs of the masses in Latin America were secondary to the need to prevent the inroads of "Soviet-controlled international communism."*

---

[14] See, for instance, President Calvin Coolidge's affirmation in Gordon Spykman, ed., *Let My People Live: Faith and Struggle in Central America* (Grand Rapids: Eerdmans, 1988), p. 111: "I have the most conclusive evidence that arms and munitions in large quantities...have been shipped to the revolutionists.... The United States cannot fail to view with deep concern any serious threat to stability and constitutional government... tending toward anarchy and jeopardizing American interests, especially if such a state of affairs is contributed to or brought about by outside influence or a foreign power."

[15] Cf. Spykman, op. cit., pp. 111-113.

The containment policy led President Eisenhower to support the CIA-sponsored invasion of Guatemala in 1954 to force out its democratically elected President, Jacobo Arbenz. Wishing to continue the reforms initiated by his predecessor, Juan Jose Arevalo,[16] Arbenz had nationalized the extensive idle lands of the United Fruit Company and compensated the U. S. company according to the values it had itself declared. His action was part of an effort to bring about an urgently needed land reform in a country where one percent of national landowners owned 40 percent of the farmland, while 88 percent of the landowners had only 14 percent of the land.[17] The United Fruit Company was the largest landholder in the country, and its income from sales in the six Central American countries doubled the regular revenues of the Guatemalan government;[18] it was to be expected that its interests would be affected by Arbenz's reforms. Secretary of State John Foster Dulles, however, regarded him as *procommunist*. Therefore, with the help of Honduras and Nicaragua, the CIA organized a covert attack, overthrew the Arbenz government, and put Colonel Carlos Castillo Armas in his place. The foreign intervention had aborted a political reform started ten years before, and inaugurated a period of state terrorism and repressive military rule which was to last for almost four decades and to produce a death toll of approximately 100,000 victims. Tellingly, in the U. S. the overthrow of the Guatemalan democratic government was called "Operation Success."[19]

---

[16] Ibid., pp. 116-117.

[17] Cf. ibid., p. 116.

[18] Idem.

[19] For a detailed account of the "Operation Success" project, see Richard H. Immerman, *The CIA in Guatemala: The Foreign Policy of Interventionism* (Austin: University of Texas Press, 1982), pp. 71-80.

The antagonism against the U. S. that (understandably) swept throughout Latin America as a result of this and similar episodes did not seem to help the U. S. government understand that *its continental "police action," based on its foreign policy of intervention, was not appreciated by a large majority of the people that such action was supposed to protect.* The situation was compounded by the triumph of Fidel Castro's guerrilla forces over the U. S.-trained troops of Cuban dictator Fulgencio Batista. Castro entered Havana on January 1, 1959. Before too long it became clear that Cuba was on its way to socialism, rapidly moving into the sphere of influence of the Soviet Union. This happening could not but confirm the need for the U. S. to increase its efforts to halt the advance of communism in order to prevent a "second Cuba." As a result, all of President Eisenhower's successors in the White House during the 60s and the 70s, except for Ford and Carter, presided over a major military intervention in Latin America. Early in his administration, in 1961, President Kennedy oversaw the Bay of Pigs invasion of Cuba using anti-Castro rebels trained by the CIA in Guatemala and Nicaragua. The invasion ended in a fiasco; its unexpected result was increased support and sympathy for the Castro regime, both within and outside Cuba. In 1965 President Johnson ordered 23,000 Marines into Santo Domingo to back up the military coup against President Juan Bosch, who had been constitutionally elected.

Now that the Pentagon papers on the CIA have been made public, it is no longer possible to deny that, under Nixon, the CIA intervened in Chile not only to prevent Allende's election as President, but also, once he was democratically elected, to destabilize his government and eventually to eliminate him—on

September 11 (!!), 1973. Thus, the U. S. government played an exceedingly important role in the establishment of Pinochet's dreadful military dictatorship, a terrorist regime, which in the succeeding years plunged thousands of Chilean families into mourning. Furthermore, there is now evidence that the same government, through its secretary for foreign affairs Henry Kissinger, cooperated in the 1970s with the military dictatorships of the Southern Cone in the so-called "Plan Cóndor," which in the name of freedom sowed violence and death in Chile, Argentina, Uruguay, and Paraguay.

The 1960s had seen the birth and demise of the Alliance for Progress, a development assistance program meant to counteract the influence of the Cuban revolution on Latin America. In March 1961, President Kennedy's speech announcing the launching of the program was received with great enthusiasm by those who believed that it was high time for the U. S. to show concern for the social and economic situation of its neighbors in practical ways. Before long, however, their hopes for change were dampened, for the Alliance for Progress turned out to be another instrument to foster U. S. security goals in the region through extensive training programs for "riot control, intelligence gathering, surveillance techniques, and psychological warfare"[20] to maintain repressive military dictatorships in power. By the end of the decade it had become clear that the basic needs that the Alliance was supposed to meet in the southern nations had been neglected once again because of the deep-seated "arrogance of power" of the U. S. and the amazing paranoia regarding the possibility of a communist takeover.

---

[20] Brian H. Smith quoted in Spykman, ibid., p. 119.

Reagan's New U. S. Inter-American Policy for the Eighties

In sharp contrast with President Carter, who had been willing to adjust U. S. foreign policy to geopolitical changes, President Ronald Reagan entered the White House in January 1981, ready to reassert U. S. dominance around the world. His foreign policy in Latin America is well illustrated by a dramatic speech he delivered to a joint session of Congress in April 1983. He described El Salvador as a country struggling for democracy but facing the communist threat represented by guerrilla forces instigated and supplied by the *Sandinista* government of Nicaragua. In line with his ambassador to the United Nations, Jeanne Kirkpatrick, who in early 1981 had declared that *"Central America is the most important place in the world for the United States,"*[21] he claimed that the national security of the Americas was at stake in Central America. And he asked the Congress to approve the granting of substantial economic and military aid to help El Salvador and to oppose Nicaragua.

This interpretation of the Central American situation in the light of "strategic globalism," and the corresponding approach to foreign policy, were defined by the so-called Santa Fe Committee in a document written in preparation for the 1980 Republican campaign.[22] According to this document, the Americas were under attack by inside and outside forces at the service of Soviet expansion. International communism was making inroads even

---

[21] Quoted in Spykman, ibid., p. 125, emphasis mine.

[22] *A New Policy for the Inter-American Relations in the Decade of the Eighties* was published by the Council for Inter-American Security, Washington, D.C., 1980.

within the U. S. sphere of influence. The time had come for the U. S. to act in order to overcome this serious threat to hemispheric security. The very survival of the U. S. as a world power demanded a new foreign policy that would take into account the close connection between external aggression and internal "subversion" in the Western hemisphere. *War, not peace, was to be the norm in international affairs.* In the face of "Soviet imperialism" the U. S. government was advised to take the initiative to keep communism out and to preserve U. S. democracy and freedom.

This "new inter-American policy for the eighties" was adopted by President Reagan as his own. In line with it, between 1981 and 1983 his administration assigned 700 million dollars to El Salvador, most of it for military training and armament. It also provided military assistance to Guatemala and Honduras, it increased military and economic aid to its allies in the Caribbean Basin, it financed anti-*Sandinista* guerrilla forces (the *contras*, based in Honduras and Costa Rica), and it actively participated in their training. As the U. S. intervention grew in Central America, however, the opposition to it also grew in Congress. In order to justify its policy, on July 19, 1983, Reagan established the National Bipartisan Commission on Central America, headed by Henry A. Kissinger. *The Report of the President's National Bipartisan Commission on Central America*[23] analyzed the economic and political crisis in Central America and made a number of recommendations on the role of the U. S. in the region. In synthesis, according to the Kissinger report, the

---

[23] Cf. *The Report of the President's National Bipartisan Commission on Central America* (New York: Macmillan Publishing Company, 1984).

problems of Central America were due to increased Soviet and Cuban influence. The demand, therefore, was for more economic aid for the region, a "substantial" increase in the level of military aid to El Salvador, and measures to meet the *Sandinista* aggression and the "security threat" that it posed to the hemisphere. One need not be an expert on Latin American issues to agree with Michael J. Kryzanek: "Although the report broke some new ground by suggesting greater emphasis on social reform and human rights protection, the major recommendations continued the traditional reliance on aid and arms as the major tools to counteract revolution."[24] That this should be the case is not surprising when it is known that in order to prepare the report the Commission spent thirty days in Washington and only nine days in foreign travel![25]

As was to be expected, the Kissinger report supplied President Reagan with justification for his foreign policy in Central America and his support for the covert war in Nicaragua, waged by the mercenary *contras*, trained and equipped by the CIA. Although Congress had succeeded in limiting the budget or the appropriation of funds for the anti-*Sandinista* rebels, the Reagan administration proved to be absolutely adamant in its objective of weakening the Nicaraguan revolution for the sake of "national security." Nicaragua took its case to the International Court, which condemned the intervention as "illegal use of force" and called on the U. S. to stop its aggression and to make indemnity payments. In response, the U. S. Government rejected the specific decision and announced that from then on it would not

---

[24] Op. cit., p. 85.
[25] See the *Report*, p. 3.

accept the competence of the Court to judge in cases such as this. Nicaragua appealed to the United Nations Security Council, but the U. S. vetoed a resolution to exhort all the nations to respect international law, even though the U. S. was not specifically named. The policy of military intervention was stubbornly applied on the assumption that the root of the problem in Central America was Soviet expansionism—that, as the Kissinger report put it, "the intrusion of aggressive outside powers exploiting local grievances to expand their own political influence and military control is a serious threat to the United States and to the entire hemisphere."[26] And the application of this policy turned Central America into a horrid military camp and an awful graveyard.

The same geopolitical considerations contained in the Kissinger report inspired the U. S. invasion of Grenada on October 25, 1983. There was evidence that beginning in 1980 Cuba and the Soviet Union had provided arms to Grenada's pro-socialist government, but there was no justification for U. S. military intervention. At first President Reagan claimed that the invasion was a rescue mission for the sake of U. S. citizens —mainly students at a local medical school—but later he admitted that the measure was taken because of the pro-Soviet stance of the regime and the threat that it posed to hemispheric security. It is, however, impossible to show how U. S. security would have been affected if the invasion had not taken place. There is no proof that the airstrip which was under construction at that time was to be used for military purposes. In contrast with the public support given to the invasion within the United States, the action was severely criticized by some of its most important

---

[26] *Report*, p. 5.

allies, including Great Britain and France, and the United States was isolated in the United Nations Security Council as the only country that voted against a resolution condemning the invasion.

In conclusion, President Reagan's "new inter-American policy for the eighties" turned out to be one more example of the well-known U. S. interventionist policy, this time placed within the framework of the East-West confrontation conceived as a cosmic struggle between Good and Evil, between Holy Democratic Capitalism and the Evil Empire. Once again Reagan showed that *the bottom line in U. S.-Latin American relations is basically defined in terms of the preservation of U. S.-made freedom and democracy in the hemisphere as an environment that openly favors U. S. economic interests regardless of the consequences for the local economy.* Whatever is inimical to that is a threat to security and must not be tolerated. Reagan proved once again the real essence of the Monroe doctrine as defined by President Woodrow Wilson's Secretary of State Robert Lassing:

> In its advocacy of the Monroe Doctrine the U. S. considers its own interests. The integrity of other American nations is an incident, not an end. While this may seem to be based on selfishness alone, the author of the Doctrine had no higher or more generous motive in its declaration.[27]

---

[27] Quoted by Noam Chomsky in *Turning the Tide: U. S. Intervention in Central America and the Struggle for Peace* (Boston: South End Press, 1985), p. 59.

II. The Tragic Effect
of U. S. Foreign Policy
in Latin America

The tragic effect of U. S. foreign policy in Latin America is the perpetuation of a socio-economic system characterized by appalling injustice. To be sure, this does not mean that the U. S. is entirely to blame for the whole deplorable situation in which over half the population of this continent lives. It does mean that *the U. S. government, for the sake of U. S. economic interests, is all too often willing to become a bed partner of the corrupt and oppressive elite that rules the Latin American countries.*

Why is Latin America Poor?

Michael Novak, the well-known representative of the neoconservative intelligentsia in the United States, has suggested that to ask about the causes of poverty is to ask the wrong question. "Poverty," he says, "is the natural condition of human beings. Poverty is what you have when you do not know causes. The question is not, what causes poverty, the question is how do you create wealth?"[28] He then goes on to answer his own question with an impressive array of arguments intended to prove that the U. S. has been able to create wealth by putting into practice the political economy proposed in 1776 by Adam Smith in his book *An Inquiry into the Nature and Causes of the Wealth of Nations.*

---

[28] Michael Novak, "Democratic Capitalism: A North American Liberation Theology," *Transformation* 2:1 (January-March, 1985): 18.

According to Novak, Smith established a contrast between the two Americas: he observed that Latin America was richer in natural resources (gold, silver, and lead) and had people "of a higher cut... many more conquistadores, aristocrats, and learned clergy," while North America was inhabited by "relatively poor dissidents, in some cases, criminals, and very few aristocrats" and had "only cotton, fur, tobacco, and corn." Nevertheless, says Novak, Smith predicted that the Latin American experiment would end in "poverty and tyranny, exactly as the liberation theologians of today describe," while the North American experiment would end in "unparalleled liberty and unprecedented prosperity."[29] The failure of the first experiment would result from the attempt to reproduce the Holy Roman Empire, with great landed estates and many landless peasants ruled by an aristocracy, with the support of the military and the clergy. By contrast, the success of the second experiment would be made possible by the power of intellect, by a political economy able to conceive a system favorable to creativity, invention, saving, and investment. Adam Smith, claims Novak, "articulated what came to be called the 'liberal vision,' liberal from the word liberate. His was the first liberation theology."[30]

What are the elements of this "liberation theology" designed by Smith to eliminate tyranny and poverty, according to our modern promoter of U. S. democracy and capitalism? At its basis is the assumption that if an order of political economy is to be built, it must be built for sinners, that is, for people who sometimes sin but most of the time are "decent, generous, and

---

[29] Ibid., p. 19.
[30] Ibid.

responsible." On the one hand, because people sometimes sin, democracy, capitalism, and pluralism are necessary: no one should be entrusted with too much power; there should be a triple system of institutions, political, economic, and moral-cultural. Tyranny will thus be prevented. On the other hand, because people most of the time are decent, generous, and responsible, democracy, capitalism, and pluralism are possible: everyone should be free to use his or her intellect to unlock the secrets of nature and to create wealth. "The cause of the wealth of nations is intellect."[31] Furthermore, "there is no such thing as a resource until the human mind has invented it. The only one, basic, natural resource is the human mind."[32] If the mind is to accomplish its task, however, it needs a free system. "The role of the political system is to empower people, to set in place the conditions—and then not to manage them."[33] Poverty will thus be eliminated.

For Novak, here lies the strength of democratic capitalism: in that it unleashes human creativity, it frees the intellect to create resources. In the final analysis, he says, "it is not nature but system and intellect that make people wealthy."[34] The implication is clear: the poor are poor because they lack both the system and the intellect which would make them wealthy. Novak does not say that in so many words; after all, his purpose is not to discuss the causes of poverty—"the most useless endeavour human beings could imagine"—,[35] but the creation of wealth. The logical

---

[31] Ibid., p. 20.

[32] Ibid., p. 21.

[33] Ibid., p. 20.

[34] Ibid., p. 21.

[35] Ibid., p. 18.

conclusion that his explanation of the causes of wealth imposes upon us, however, is that poverty results from the absence of those two elements that have created wealth under democratic capitalism. And the solution, according to the North American liberation theologian, is not political activism and socialist revolution, as Latin American liberation theologians maintain, but the liberal revolution, "the only revolution that has a theory about institutions designed for sinful human beings during the long days after the revolution."[36] To conclude, he asks: "Which institutions actually raise up the poor? Which institutions actually do protect human rights?" And he responds: "Let people try as many experiments as they wish, but only under one condition: that they be honest about what works and what does not work, and change accordingly."[37]

Novak's response, however, raises in turn another set of questions: For whom does democratic capitalism work? If it does not work for everybody, how does it affect those for whom it does not work? Honesty demands not to take for granted that a system designed for people to become wealthy is equally beneficial to all, or that intellect is not being used by the strong to take advantage of the weak. Since all human beings are sinners, it may well be that the very same system and the very same intellect which make some people wealthy make many others—the large majority, in fact—poor!

Colonial Structures

Novak may not be interested in analyzing the causes of poverty, but he has put his finger on one of the main reasons for

---

[36] Ibid., p. 23.
[37] Ibid., p. 22.

it in Latin America: the presence of a landed aristocracy that, in conjunction with the military and oftentimes the Roman Catholic clergy, rules over the large majority of people. What he does not see is the connection between that wealthy elite and the expanding worldwide economic system into which the region was incorporated beginning at the end of the fifteenth century.

In fact, the Spanish and Portuguese conquest and colonization left behind a legacy of economic structures heavily dependent on export agriculture and raw materials, geared to benefit a privileged elite. That legacy is still there. Labor and land control and political power continue to be in the hands of a small group of powerful and wealthy families.[38] The independence from Spain and Portugal achieved by the Latin American countries in the nineteenth century left the unjust socioeconomic structures of colonial times untouched. The new governments did very little or nothing to change the relationship between the rich and the poor. Independence meant that the wealthy elite now had the freedom to establish new links with foreign investors, without Spanish or Portuguese interference. The net result was the consolidation of "internal colonialism", a system of exploitation until quite recently legitimized by Roman Catholic Christendom.

A sad illustration of the way in which the prevailing colonial system has affected the majority of people is the situation of land tenure in Central America:

> Repeatedly the question of "whose land?" has been answered to the advantage of the elite. Peasants and small

---

[38] This, however, is changing in practically all the Latin American countries, where the land is increasingly becoming a possession of big international agribusiness.

landowners have progressively been forced off their little plots and communal lands. Rights to land by use have not been recognized, and titles have not been granted. Efforts to reclaim family and traditional properties have frequently been met with violence and repression.[39]

As a result, millions of landless peasants have been forced to choose one of three options: to move to a region near a fruit plantation or a cattle farm, quite likely owned by a foreign company in complicity with the local oligarchy; to migrate to an already over-crowded city where few jobs and little housing are available, or to go to *"el Norte"* to join the thousands of Central American refugees in one of the neighboring countries or in the United States.[40]

This is institutionalized violence. Unfortunately, as Noam Chomsky has put it, "the violence of everyday life in the area of influence and control of the U. S. is not considered a topic of interest except at moments when it threatens the established order."[41]

Economic Dependence

Advocates of the free-market enterprise like Michael Novak simply assume that what Latin America needs to solve its problem of poverty is a democratic capitalist system to allow the human mind to create wealth. Economic growth or development is for them the natural result of Adam Smith's political economy. The fact is, however, that capitalist economic development in

---

[39] Spykman, op. cit., pp. 74-75.

[40] Cf. ibid., pp. 75-80.

[41] Op. cit., p. 7.

Latin America has failed to produce the intended results but has rather brought with it a whole series of unintended tragic results.

Brazil—the "sleeping giant"—is a case in point. In the early seventies, under the authoritarian government of General Emilio Medici, one the major figures of the 1964 military revolution, Brazil experienced what came to be known as an "economic miracle." Steered by Delfim Neto, the economic growth reached its highest level since the fifties, with the industrial sector taking the lead with an annual growth of 12.6 percent. Brazil was on the move, and economists and planners arrived from all over the world to learn its secret. The euphoria did not last too long, however. As President Medici himself commented in 1970: "The economy is going fine, but the people aren't."[42] To be sure, the economic pie was now bigger than ever, but the technocrats had overlooked the fact that the production of the pie involved debts that had to be serviced. In 1974 alone, under the impact of OPEC's price shock, Brazil had to borrow abroad to such an extent that its foreign debt increased from $6.2 billion to $11.9 billion. By 1978 the foreign debt had risen to $43.5 billion.[43] The net result of the Brazilian "miracle" was a country with one of the most unequal income distributions in the world, where the highest 20 percent of the households received more than 60 percent of the total household income,[44] and where agricultural policy favored increased production of export crops (primarily soybeans, cotton, and wheat) but allowed production of the

---

[42] Quoted by Chomsky, op. cit., p. 159.

[43] Thomas E. Skidmore, *The Politics of Military Rule in Brazil, 1964-85* (New York: Oxford University Press, 1988), pp. 180, 207.

[44] Ibid., p. 284.

staples of the popular diet (rice and beans, as in Central America) to fall.[45]

How can it be that countries that export food are unable to feed their own population? Obviously, rapid economic growth does not automatically improve the situation of the poor. As Alencar Furtado wrote in 1972, in the middle of the Brazilian economic "miracle": "We live in an economy that benefits the few while sacrificing the millions."[46]

The basic problem with the modernization projects of dependent capitalism is that they are inserted into an international economic system characterized by injustice. They are not part and parcel of the national productive structures. Rather, they represent "an alien 'modernity' whose internal dynamics are determined by distant and often unknown actors and objectives which are frequently opposed to Latin American countries' national interests."[47] These modernization projects involve increased spending, and increased spending in Latin America has been met, not by internal economic output, foreign trade or higher levels of taxation, but by increased borrowing. Eager to invest the flush of petrodollars made available by the OPEC countries as a result of higher oil prices in the early 1970s, the banks found the Latin American governments all too ready to accept loans to further their economic development.

---

[45] Ibid., p. 299.

[46] Quoted by Skidmore, ibid., p. 143.

[47] Fernando Fainzylber. "Democratization, Endogenous Modernization, and Integration: Strategic Choices for Latin America and Economic Relations with the United States," in Kevin J. Middlebrook and Carlos Rico, eds., The United States and Latin America in the 1980s (Pittsburgh: University of Pittsburgh Press, 1986), p. 134.

Unfortunately, increased loans bring with them increased interest and service charges on the debts. The picture becomes even darker due to the following negative economic factors, which can only be mentioned here: (a) the terms of trade in the exchange of agricultural products for manufactured goods; (b) the floating interest rates; (c) the austerity programs required by the International Monetary Fund as a condition for receiving loans; (d) the reduction of imports for internal industries when the balance of trade is unfavorable; (e) the devaluation of national currencies in relation to the dollar, with the resulting increase of the debt in dollars; (f) the reduction of public funds and the consequent cutbacks in fiscal spending.[48] All these factors, compounded with the entrenched and heartless corruption that has traditionally marred politics in Latin America,[49] have plunged these countries into a deep gorge of poverty and hopelessness, with foreign debts that undermine every prospect for a better future.

As a matter of fact, since the middle of the 1970s the foreign debt, now exceeding the sum of $800 billion, has become the most eloquent expression of Latin America's economic dependence and one of the most serious threats to its political

---

[48] Cf. Spykman, op. cit., pp. 94-96.

[49] For a balanced view of the Latin American situation, it must be observed that corruption in this region, as in many other regions of the world, especially among politicians and business people, creates innumerable loopholes that foreign powers, such as the Citibank, IBM, and the U. S. government, exploit to their own advantage. For an incisive and well-documented analysis of U. S. participation in the business of corruption in Latin America, see Andrés Oppenheimer, *Ojos vendados: Estados Unidos y el negocio de la corrupción en América Latina* (Buenos Aires: Editorial Sudamericana, 2001).

stability. The 1988 News Report of the Inter-American Development Bank described the onset of the debt as "the key event of the region's recent economic history."[50] Despite the "emergence" of Latin America in the 1970s—when its international and intra-regional ties were extended and diversified—, *all the countries in the region, regardless of their political position, are now deeply affected by this crisis that places them in a condition of complete subordination to foreign interests.* The U. S. plays a special role in this crisis not only because a very high percentage of the debt is owed to U. S.-based commercial banks, but also because the U. S. government controls the international financial institutions such as the World Bank and the International Monetary Fund,[51] interest rates, and trade policies. Thinking of the 1980s, Laurence Whitehead wrote:

> Developing countries that "normally" supplemented their domestic savings with foreign capital inflows now find themselves abruptly compelled to generate export surpluses to repay capital to their industrialized country creditors—and, in effect, to finance the U. S. budget deficit.... The net resource transfer from Latin America to the industrialized countries (in fact, overwhelmingly to the United States) was estimated at $20 billion in 1982 and $30 billion in 1983. These totals did not include unrecorded capital flight, which was probably of comparable dimensions. The decapitalization of Latin America continued during 1984,

---

[50] Inter-American Development Bank News, 1988.

[51] On the negative role that these institutions play in relation to the economy of the poor countries, see Joseph E. Stiglitz, Nobel Prize Recipient in Economics 2001, *El malestar en la globalización* (Buenos Aires: Taurus, 2002). Only the Spanish translation available to the author.

driven by the lure of high U. S. interest rates and political insecurity and rampant inflation in Latin America.[52]

Since then the situation has been seriously aggravated by the market fundamentalism that, under the aegis of economic development, has become the hallmark of today's global economic system. As a result, the Latin American countries have become net exporters of capital to the wealthy countries, especially to the United States. The tragic consequences that this anomaly is having on their internal economy can hardly be exaggerated. The demand to stave off external default becomes the top priority, inflation often reaches unprecedented levels everywhere, and every other need is postponed—gross domestic product, employment, food, housing, health, education, salaries.

The dream to modernize Latin America by the creation of wealth through the free market system and the use of the intellect has turned into a nightmare. But democratic capitalism is not what Novak makes it out to be in the United States either. Managed by its conservative advocates, in the last few years it has succeeded in increasing the gap between the rich and the poor within this country in an appalling way. The country is ruled by what Chomsky has called "a highly class conscious business community" that controls the state according to its interests, while ordinary people are excluded from sustained participation in the political processes. Needless to say, propaganda plays a crucial role within this framework. Today's managers of the system and

---

[52] "Debt, Diversification, and Dependency: Latin America's International Political Relations", in Kevin J. Middlebrook and Carlos Rico, eds., *The United States and Latin America in the 1980s* (Pittsburgh: University of Pittsburgh Press, 1986), p. 97.

the intellect would agree with Edward Bernays, member of the government propaganda commission during World War I, who in the 1920s wrote:

> The conscious and intelligent manipulation of the organized habits and opinions of the masses is an important element in democratic society... it is the intelligent minorities which need to make use of propaganda continuously and systematically. In the active proselytizing of minorities in whom selfish interests and public interests coincide lie the progress and development of America.[53]

The forgoing discussion should be sufficient to show the inadequacy of asking how to create wealth without at the same time asking how to distribute it—how to insure that the wealth created does not benefit the few who manage the system and the intellect for their own gain in detriment of the large majorities.

Economics and the Militarization of Latin America

U. S. foreign policy in Latin America is based on the assumption that there is an inter-American system constituted by nations that share the same ideals and interests and are therefore under the moral obligation to cooperate with one another and with the whole region. But how does this assumption square with the principle of self-determination and freedom which is part and parcel of the U. S. democratic tradition? It does not, and it does not have to, because from the perspective of U. S. policymakers the Latin American countries are free but are morally obliged to serve common interests. On the other hand, the U. S. is also

---

[53] Quoted by Chomsky, *Turning the Tide*, p. 235.

obliged to help those countries to become truly free and able to fulfill their commitments within the hemisphere. According to the Kissinger *Report*, "When our neighbors are in trouble, we cannot close our eyes and still be true to ourselves."[54]

In light of this kind of generosity, how can we Latin Americans cast doubts on the motivations behind all the diligence that North Americans display when our freedom is threatened by any form of conspiracy from outside or of subversion from within? How can we disagree with their noble efforts to maintain order and stability in the region for the sake of its economic development?

From this perspective, it is not surprising that since the middle of this century the United States has channeled into Latin America hundreds of millions of dollars in training and supplies through the Military Assistance Program (MAP).[55] If economic development is to take place, so the argument goes, stability must be guaranteed and every possibility of subversion must be averted by force. In more concrete terms this means that priority must be given to the building up of a powerful "security" system—powerful enough to keep the subversives out so that the local "democratic" capitalist entrepreneurs and foreign business corporations are able to do their job of creating wealth which will eventually "trickle down" to the masses. Thus, economic development provides the justification for the security system that at present determines so much of the U. S. foreign policy.

Security for the sake of economic development provided the rationale for the establishment of a "National Security State"

---

[54] Kissinger, *Report*, p. 2.

[55] The largest military aid provided by the United States goes to Colombia, a country with a poor record with regard to human rights.

(NSS), with the support of the United States, in several Latin American countries during the 1970s and 1980s. The NSS derived its logic from the confrontation between the United States and the Soviet Union in what was known as the Cold War. Each superpower was committed to maintaining stability within its own sphere of influence. This involved not only domestic militarization and propaganda against the enemy's aggression in order to justify the costs of military expenditures, but also all kinds of security measures to avert instability abroad. As a result, "The two superpowers [were] locked into military systems of domestic social and economic management and global domination."[56]

Within the U. S. the NSS took the form of what Bertram Gross called "friendly fascism,"[57] committed to the use of state power and state violence in defense of business and financial interests. Chomsky has summarized the effects of this approach to politics, especially under the Reagan administration, on the labor movement, civil rights, environmental protection, independent thought, political parties, and the public mind.[58] As a result, democracy in the U. S. has been effectively limited to the possibility of participating in so-called "democratic elections." A large percentage of the population has been seduced through the mass media by the powerful industrial-military complex; they are basically indifferent to ideas or actions which transcend their private life, including, of course, questions of U. S. foreign policy. How can democracy flourish in this environment? As Chomsky has put it,

---

[56] Chomsky, *Turning the Tide*, p. 217.

[57] *Friendly Fascism* (Boston: South Bend Press, 1983).

[58] *Turning the Tide*, pp. 221-237.

Meaningful democracy presupposes the ability of ordinary people to pool their limited resources, to form and develop ideas and programs, put them on the political agenda, and act to support them. In the absence of organizational structures and resources that make this possible, democracy amounts to the option of choosing among candidates who represent the interests of one or another group that has an independent power base, generally in the private economy.[59]

In the United States the NSS has had a domesticating effect on the population. The consequences of this kind of State, however, have been even more tragic in Latin America, including the "disappearance" of thousands and thousands of people[60] and the unscrupulous violation of human rights. The methods used by the NSS to create a system of intimidation and repression—including modern forms of torture that go far beyond those of Nazi Germany—in order to prevent any way of thinking or acting which does not follow the official line has been amply documented in various countries.[61] The connection between the NSS and U. S. business interests is clearly illustrated by the participation of ITT in the overthrow of President Salvador Allende in Chile in 1973. When it became clear that the election of a socialist government was a real possibility, Harold Geneen, the chairman of ITT, asked the CIA to join hands with the company in order to prevent Allende's election. The CIA declined, primarily because the U. S. ambassador in Chile,

---

[59] *Turning the Tide*, p. 221.

[60] Cf. Edward S. Herman, *The Real Terror Network: Terrorism in Fact and Propaganda* (Boston: South End Press, 1982).

[61] On Argentina, where approximately 30,000 people disappeared during the military dictatorship (1976-1982), see *Nunca más* (Buenos Aires: CONADEP, 1985).

Edward Korry, was strongly opposed to covert government-business alliances. Geneen, however, persisted in his effort and contacted the CIA chief for clandestine operations in Latin America with the offer to make a substantial contribution to the campaign of the conservative candidate, Jorge Alessandri. The CIA official rejected the plan but ITT went ahead and provided $350,000 in covert political assistance to Alessandri. Once Allende was elected, ITT also channeled funds to conservative newspaper *El Mercurio* to campaign against him.[62]

The ideology of the NSS was also behind the covert war against Nicaragua during the *Sandinista* government in that country. President Reagan, who "repeatedly argued that the incomplete application of military power was the reason for the loss of the Vietnam War,"[63] provided military aid to Honduras and El Salvador to stop the "insurrection" within their respective borders and subsidized the *Contras*—heirs of dictator Somoza´s National Guard—to stop the "Nicaraguan threat" through "low intensity conflict."[64] As a result Honduras became militarily-occupied territory, a base for the training of North American soldiers and for the *Contra* operation; El Salvador was trapped into a violent vicious circle of insurgence and anti-insurgence, and Nicaragua was cornered in a war with a death toll of 70,000 people and became the poorest country in the Americas with the

---

[62] Cf. Seymour Hersh, "The Price of Power: Kissinger, Nixon and Chile," *The Atlantic*, Dec. 1982.

[63] Robert Jewett & John Shelton Lawrence, op. cit., p. 117.

[64] According to Spykman *et al*, the "low-intensity conflict" is "a doctrine of warfare applied mainly in Third World regions, such as Central America, where fighting is done by local proxy armies and the war is aimed at the entire grass-roots population" (op. cit., p. 269).

exception of Haiti. Paradoxically enough, according to U. S. foreign policy the purpose of the covert war against the Central American country was to bring to it the freedom and democracy that it lacked!

According to Article 20 of the Charter of the Organization of American States, "The territory of a state is inviolable; it may not be the object, even temporarily, of military occupation or of other measures of force taken by another state, directly or indirectly, on any grounds whatever...."[65] This is why the Latin American response to the Central American crisis in the 1980s was in terms of a multilateral diplomatic process led by the so-called *Contadora* group. Initially formed by Colombia, Mexico, Panama and Venezuela, this group proposed a plan for establishing peace and democracy in Central America by reducing foreign military personnel, ending subversion, stopping the flow of weapons and achieving a regional peace treaty.

What kind of hearing did this group have in Washington? The response of the U. S. government to this peace initiative coming from Latin America was colored by the Kissinger *Report*:

> The Contadora nations do not have extensive experience in working together, and the Contadora process has not been tested in terms of crafting specific policies to provide for regional security. Thus the United States cannot use the Contadora process as a substitute for its own policies. Experience has shown that the process works most effectively when the United States acts purposefully. When our policy stagnates, the Contadora process languishes. When we are decisive, the Contadora process gathers momentum.[66]

---

[65] Quoted by Spykman *et al,* op. cit., p. 163.

[66] Kissinger *Report*, pp. 142-34.

In other words, we are in charge, we have experience, we have defined the real problem and we know the answer, and the success or failure of whatever is done depends on us! Notwithstanding, concludes the *Report*, "The Contadora countries are engaged in a bold new experiment. They deserve the gratitude and encouragement of all the nations of the hemisphere."[67]

Despite the "bold new experiment," the *Contra* war kept going. Not only that, but in July 1986 President Reagan managed to get Congressional approval of $100 million in military aid to the *Contras*. And in November the world was startled at the news scandal that, before the July Congress approval, the U. S. National Security Council had circumvented congressional restrictions on *Contra* aid and had secretly obtained funds from other sources.

Diplomacy may not sound very attractive to politicians who realize that accepting it would mean limiting the exercise of power in countries which they regard as their backyard. There is, however, a very high cost involved in maintaining peace without justice. And as Kryzanek has stated, U. S. leaders may find that "making adjustments to the new power realities may be ultimately more attractive than sending invasion forces or maintaining covert operations."[68]

Is Democracy Viable in Latin America?

According to Kryzanek, "the fragile support for democracy" in Latin America is due to the lack of a democratic tradition and the

---

[67] Ibid.

[68] Op. cit., p. 213.

predominance of an authoritarian heritage.[69] That problem is real but it is not equally present in all Latin American countries. Chile, for instance, had a long, well-established democratic tradition before Pinochet's military coup. The one common factor that does conspire against democracy in all the southern republics, however, is a growing social unrest created by the increasing impoverishment of the masses.

Take the case of Brazil, for example. When Jose Sarney was sworn in as President on April 22, 1985, he inherited from the military government not only a staggering debt but also a credit crisis that had reached its lowest point already in 1982, when new loans to service previous loans ran out. "The bill to be paid," says Skidmore, "was of a level to make any prudent banker shudder. Merely paying interest on its debt in 1985 caused Brazil to export capital at the rate of 5 percent of GDP. Few economists believe any developing country can long continue exporting capital at such a rate. Such 'foreign aid' is bound to stir a reaction at home."[70] Shortly after his inauguration Sarney wrote:

> I, without wishing it, without having any time to prepare myself for it, became the holder of the largest foreign debt on the face of the earth, as well as the greatest interest debt. My inheritance included the deepest recession in our history, the highest rate of unemployment, an unprecedented climate of violence, political disintegration and the highest rate of inflation ever recorded in our country's history—250 percent, with the prospect of reaching 1,000 percent.[71]

---

[69] Op. cit., p. 153.

[70] Op. cit., p. 307.

[71] Quoted by Skidmore, ibid., p. 261.

With minor changes here and there, this dark description of Brazil could be applied to every Latin American country. During the late 1970s and early 1980s, the whole region saw the successive replacement of military regimes by civilian governments. The internal problems compounded with the heavy burden imposed by the transfer of resources for the sake of servicing the foreign debt, however, resulted in a sharp decline in GDP in all the Latin American countries.[72] Consequently, most democratic governments in Latin America are finding it increasingly difficult to face the social pressures created by crippling inflation rates and shrinking economies. Injustice is the order of the day in the Americas, and injustice carries within it the seed of subversion. Unless the oppressive economic situation of the Latin American masses is drastically changed within the next few years, the southern republics will inevitably find themselves involved in waves of popular rage that no government will be able to control. That being the case, the greatest threat to democracy all over the continent is not terrorism but the greed of a privileged and corrupt elite who, in connivance with business corporations protected by U. S. foreign policy, are able to manipulate the socioeconomic and political system to their own advantage.

---

[72] Regarding the first few years of the 1980s—the so-called "lost decade" for Latin America—Fajnsylber writes: "Regional GDP fell by 1.0 percent in 1982 and 3.1 percent in 1983, rising to only an estimated 2.6 percent in 1984. Per capita GDP fell continuously from 1981 through 1983, with a cumulative decline of 8.9 percent from 1981 through 1984. Urban unemployment and inflation increased significantly throughout Latin America" (op. cit., p. 152).

III. Peace as the Fruit of Justice

Our survey of the history of U. S.-Latin American relations has clearly shown that the U. S. appeal to "security" is a way to rationalize, and the militarization of Latin America is a way to secure, favorable conditions to exploit human and natural resources for the benefit of the powerful. In light of that history, there is no exaggeration in saying that the war in Iraq represents one more instance of the state terrorism that has been part and parcel of U. S. foreign policy ever since the United States became a world power.

Fulbright wrote *The Price of Empire* shortly before the fall of the Soviet empire. One of the purposes of his book was to encourage the two super-powers—the United States and the Soviet Union—, the protagonists of the Cold War, to set aside their mutual rivalry and the consequent arms race. Both of these great powers, he wrote, "are engaging, in reality, in quite similar activities in third-world countries to promote their ideas of how to organize society."[73] And to surpass the rival, each one was involved in great military expenditures that threatened their economic stability. *For both of them the time was ripe for radical change in the manner of thinking with regard to foreign relations.* "The key question," said the distinguished U. S. Senator, "is the willingness of both sides to engage in peaceful competition—to put ideology to the only test that counts, the test of which system [socialism or capitalism] can produce a better life for its people."[74]

---

[73] Op. cit., p. 20.
[74] Ibid., p. 33.

The fall of the Berlin Wall marked the end of the Cold War, but not of imperialistic expansion, no longer of two super-powers, but of only one. From then on the globalization of capitalism would take place without any kind of competition. The "balance of power", which had been a matter of concern during the Cold War years, became a "balance" imposed by the triumphant super-power—a balance maintained by the hegemonic power of money, a power which defines every type of relationship, including international relations.

The document on the strategy for National Security issued in 1999 by the U. S. National Security Council does not hide the intentions of the U. S. government with regard to the use of violence in order to protect U. S. economic interests. It defines these "vital interests" in terms of "the physical security of our allies; the security of our citizens; our economic well-being;" it affirms the purpose to "knock down the commercial barriers abroad in order to create jobs in the country," and it concludes: "We will do whatever is necessary to defend our interests. We would even use our military power in a unilateral and decisive way, if that were necessary."[75] *The war in Iraq demonstrates that the U. S. government is quite ready to implement that policy even if all the arguments to go to war are proved to be false.*

Quite clearly, Fulbright's call for a U. S. international policy based on peace and the common search for the well-being of all people everywhere is still relevant today. Sadly, U. S. foreign policy continues to be controlled by its economic interests. No-one should be surprised, therefore, that all around the world

---

[75] Quoted by Luis Bilbao, "Estados Unidos alista un ejército para el ALCA," *Le Monde Diplomatique,* 3:27 (September2001), p. 6. Only the Spanish translation available to the author.

resentment and even hatred against the U. S.—the paradigm of the capitalist world—grows like a plague. To a large extent, present-day globalization is the globalization of a "savage capitalism" that fosters injustice and inequity, excludes hundreds of thousands from the labor market, and condemns millions of families to poverty and even misery. Add to this the U. S. policy of support for the State of Israel over against the Palestinian claims to the land, and you have all the ingredients for the awful platter that a group of fanatical Arabs placed on the U. S. table on September 11, 2001.

U. S. foreign policy, severely criticized by one of its most lucid analysts, does not *justify* but does *explain* the horrible terrorist act. This atrocity shows that terrorism has become a highly sophisticated citizen of a globalized world. From a Christian perspective, every form of terrorism, including both the one that invokes Allah and the one inspired by Mammon, is repugnant. The challenge that it poses before us as Christians is to proclaim in both word and deed, with greater dedication than ever before, the Good News of universal validity—the Gospel of the Prince of Peace. The word of the prophet Isaiah remains as relevant today as it was in his own day: "The fruit of justice will be peace; the effect of justice will be quietness and confidence forever" (Is 32:17).

4

Materialism and Ethnocentric Patriotism: Twin Idolatries

What does it profit a man to gain the whole world and lose his soul?
(Matthew 16:26)

The love of money is the root of all evil.
(I Timothy 6:10)

Do not suppose that you can say to yourselves,
'We have Abraham for our father;'
for I say to you, that God is able from these stones
to raise up children of Abraham.
(Matthew 3:9)

To announce that there must be no criticism of the President,
or that we are to stand by the President, right or wrong,
is not only unpatriotic and servile, but is morally treasonable
to the American public.
(Theodore Roosevelt, 1918)

Sincere Christians should not deliberately accept any commitment that would weaken or distort their relationship to Jesus Christ. Nevertheless, the Bible is clear that some Christians, because of commitments that conflict with their Christian faith, do indeed drift away from God. Loyalties to people, to organizations and to created objects have the possibility not only of weakening our walk with God, but at times they can even turn into idolatry. Evangelical voices from Latin America suggest that churches in the United States are coming under the power of two idolatries: materialism and ethnocentric patriotism. Bolivian Methodist Bishop Mortimer Arias acknowledges that although the social gospel of mainline Protestantism, the individualistic gospel of North American evangelicals, and the pentecostal version of the good news contain some Biblical truth, all three are reductions of the original gospel and omit important aspects.[1] Peruvian missiologist Samuel Escobar notes that the geographical base of the Church has moved south from Europe and North America to Latin America, Asia, and Africa. The vibrancy of these *poor* churches raises the question whether the affluent message proclaimed in the *First World* really is faithful to the Word of God.[2] Brazilian Assembly of God pastor Ricardo Gondim claims that North American Christians have become worldly and have been molded into the image of their culture. For many evangelicals in the United States, "the 'American way of life' and the gospel are Siamese twins. It is almost impossible to separate them."[3] These accusations are quite serious. If they are true, then Christians in the United States are more influenced in their actions by these idols than they are by Christ and Scripture. Therefore, U. S. evangelical support for the war in Iraq might have been grounded more in non-Christian ideas than in the Bible. These Latin American church leaders urge their North American brothers and sisters to search the Scriptures to see if these accusations are true. With that in mind we will look at the

---

[1] Mortimer Arias, *Announcing the Reign of God: Evangelization and the Subversive Memory of Jesus* (Philadelphia: Fortress Press, 1984).

[2] Samuel Escobar, *Changing Tides: Latin America & World Mission Today* (New York: Orbis, 2002).

[3] Ricardo Gondim in *"Pastor cuestiona la importación de modelos evangélicos"* in *Servicios de Noticias ALC*: November 1, 2002.

Biblical understanding of these idolatries and their pernicious effects upon the witness of the Church. We will also explore contemporary North American culture as well as the evangelical sub-culture to see if North American Christians are falling under their power.

Materialism in the Bible

Jesus talked a lot about money! But He did not encourage his followers to spend large quantities of money on church building projects nor on extravagant mission trips. He urged them to share their money and other possessions with those in need. He also warned them about the dangers of money upon their own lives.

In his well-known parable of the seed and the sower[4] Jesus describes various responses to the gospel message. He utilizes four types of "earthy responses:" the road, the rocky soil, the land with thorns, and the good earth, to illustrate four general types of human reactions to the gospel. In this parable the land with thorns represents believers who want to become affluent. Although they initially respond very well to the good news, they end up fruitless because "the deceitfulness of riches and the desires for other things enter in and choke the word, and it becomes unfruitful" (Mark 4:19). Luke's version emphasizes that riches are deceitful, misleading people into believing falsehoods. Jesus' words clearly show that this tragic unfruitfulness occurs among those who profess an initial belief, even among those who seem to be quite fervent in their faith. If the cares and riches and pleasures of first century Judean peasant life could choke the

---

[4] Matthew 13:1-23; Mark 4:1-20; and Luke 8:1-15.

word and make it unfruitful, then it is likely that a similar, but even more damaging, fruit-inhibiting process is taking place within the richest country that the world has ever known, the United States of the twenty-first century.

If it is possible for the thorns to choke out the gospel, it is important for us to reexamine the Scriptures and identify clearly that original gospel message and then compare it with our own contemporary proclamation of it. Jesus came proclaiming the reign or kingdom of God. It was a God-centered message. God, in the person of His Son Jesus Christ, was demonstrating His reign upon earth and calling people to submit to His authority: "The time is fulfilled, and the kingdom of God is at hand; repent and believe in the gospel."[5] People were urged to turn away from their sins and experience the life-giving changes promised by the Lord.

At certain times, multitudes responded enthusiastically to this message, but they were not always sincere. John the Baptist recognized that many Judeans who came to be baptized were, in fact, not willing to turn from their sins. He demanded that they demonstrate their sincerity with "fruits in keeping with repentance." When probed what these fruits were, he answered, *"Let the person who has two tunics share with the one who has none; and let the person who has food do likewise."* Specific instructions were given to the tax collectors: "Don't collect any more than you are required to." A similar exhortation was given to the soldiers: "Don't extort money and don't accuse people falsely—be content with your pay." Although John the Baptist goes from a general exhortation to more specific instructions, it

---

[5] Mark 1:15; see also Matthew 4:17; 10:7.

is important to note that each command dealt with money or possessions and with the treatment of one's neighbor. True repentance towards God, even for average people of first-century Judea, involved turning away from the idolatry of materialism and treating others as we would treat God Himself. Luke concludes that these exhortations for repentance were part and parcel of preaching the gospel.[6]

Examples from the life and ministry of Jesus demonstrate that He continued and extended the practice of John the Baptist. Jesus did not water down the gospel message in order to attract more followers. A rich, young ruler came to Jesus seeking salvation.[7] The young man believed that he had kept all the commandments of God. Jesus told him, "One thing you lack. *Go sell everything you have and give it to the poor, and you will have treasure in heaven. Then come, follow me.*" (Mark 10:21). The young man went away sad, because he had many possessions. Jesus did not run after the man to try and persuade him. Jesus could have reduced his command, perhaps by just asking the youth to sell 10% of his possessions, but Jesus did not do that. He did not make the message easier by lowering His standards. Jesus had shown that the rich young man was committing idolatry, by having sold his soul to his possessions. F. F. Bruce argues persuasively that Jesus' instruction to the young man was not an isolated case, but rather a regular feature of His teaching. After comparing this passage with Luke 19:1-10 and Luke 12:33-34 Bruce concludes, "Jesus' words to him were not

---

[6] Luke 3:7-18, especially verse 18. The original Greek text clarifies that the exhortations to repentance were an essential part of the gospel, "With many other words John exhorted the people and preached the good news to them."

[7] Matthew 19:16-30; Mark 10:17-30; Luke 18:18-30.

intended for him alone, they remain as a challenge, a challenge not to be evaded, for all who wish to be his disciples."[8]

Jesus used this episode to teach his followers an important, yet astonishing truth. He told them, "How hard it is for the rich to enter the kingdom of God!" His disciples were shocked. Jesus repeated, "How hard it is to enter the kingdom of God! *It is easier for a camel to go through the eye of a needle than for a rich man to enter the kingdom of God*" (Mark 10:23-25). Down through the centuries, but especially in the twentieth century, commentators have looked for creative interpretations of this passage that would reduce the harshness of Jesus' words.[9] Probably the best interpretation is to recognize that Jesus was using a hyperbole "to drive the lesson home; it is impossible for a rich man to enter the kingdom of God—humanly impossible, Jesus concedes, for God, with whom nothing is impossible, can even save a rich man. But if so, then the rich man's heart must be changed, by having its attachment to material riches replaced by attachment to the true riches, 'treasure in heaven.'"[10]

---

[8] F. F. Bruce, *The Hard Sayings of Jesus* (Downers Grove, IL: InterVarsity Press, 1983), pp. 174-177.

[9] Some suggest that the original word "kamilos" (=cable) was modified to "kamélos" (=camel), thus the original should be rendered "a rope to go through the eye of a needle". Perhaps the most common homiletical interpretation is that a camel had to get down on its knees to enter the small "eye of a needle" gate in Jerusalem. Therefore we too must get on our knees to come into God's kingdom. There is no archaeological evidence to support the "eye of a needle" gate in Jerusalem. Bruce, *Hard Sayings*, p. 183, claims, "There is probably no saying of Jesus which is 'harder' in the Western mind today than the saying about the camel and the needle's eye, none which carries with it such a strong temptation to tone it down."

[10] Ibid., 182.

Jesus considered wealth to be an idol, a powerful force that he called Mammon. Mammon exercised powers over those who served it. Jesus warned that it was impossible to serve God and to serve Mammon at the same time.[11] In the Sermon on the Mount Jesus urged His disciples not to lay up treasure on earth. Their hearts would follow their treasures. Jesus recognized that Mammon so dominated people's lives that they spent most of their time seeking after food, drink and clothing. Although these are valid needs, God will provide enough for His followers. True disciples should seek first and foremost God's reign and God's justice.[12]

According to Luke's gospel, Jesus repeated his warning about the idolatry of Mammon in the presence of the Pharisees. Luke tells us that in addition to being very religious, the Pharisees were also "lovers of money" and were scoffing at Jesus (Luke 16:14). The Lord rebuked them and said, "You are the ones who justify yourselves in the eyes of men, but God knows your hearts. What is highly valued among men is detestable in God's sight." (Luke 16:15). The Pharisees, who generally possessed orthodox doctrine, had come under the blinding spell of Mammon. Their doctrinal self-righteousness was concomitant with their love for money. They were not even aware that their practices were detestable in the sight of God. Jesus then told them the story about the rich man and poor Lazarus. The rich man died and

---

[11] Matthew 6:24. The Apostle Paul concurs, for he identifies greed as idolatry in Colossians 3:5.

[12] Matt. 6:19-33. The Greek word *dikaiosune* is much better translated *justice* than *righteousness* in modern English. See Lindy Scott, "North American Christians and the Latin American Church: Lessons from South of the Border," The Network for Strategic Missions. http://www.strategic network.org/index.php?loc=kb&page=detail&id=3126

was tormented in Hades, whereas Lazarus entered into eternal life (Luke 16:19-31). Jesus was not affirming that all poor people go to heaven nor that all rich people go to hell.[13] Nevertheless, if a rich person does not eagerly share with those in need, it should be questioned if that person really knows the God and Father of Jesus.

Perhaps the most haunting words coming from Jesus are these: "What does it profit a man to gain the whole word and lose his own soul?"[14] In no uncertain terms, Jesus called his disciples to an uncompromising allegiance to him. The accumulation of wealth could be very, very dangerous. Not only could material goods weaken a person's relationship with God, they could entirely cut a person off from God.

The early church in the New Testament provides numerous examples of Christians who were set free from the idolatry of money as well as a few negative examples of those who gave in to Mammon. On the day of Pentecost, the Spirit came upon the newborn church in a dramatic way. Luke describes the powerful impact of the Spirit upon the believers as they dedicated themselves to the apostles' teaching, fellowship, the breaking of bread and prayer. *"All the believers were together and had everything in common. Selling their possessions and goods, they gave to anyone as he had need"* (Acts 2:44-45). The true demonstration of Christian fellowship is sharing with those in

---

[13] Good hermeneutical practice rightfully requires that difficult passages be interpreted in the light of clearer ones. Salvation is based upon God's grace, not upon one's poverty nor good works. Nevertheless, one's actions do express the presence or absence of God's saving grace in a person's life. See Ephesians 2:8-10.

[14] Matthew 16:26; Mark 8:36; Luke 9:25.

need.[15] God's blessing was upon this new community of faith and He added to their numbers daily.

The Spirit of God continued to guide the community of faith through times of growth, miracles, and persecutions from the Sanhedrin. Luke again describes how the church had been set free from Mammon's control.

> All the believers were one in heart and mind. *No one claimed that any of his possessions was his own, but they shared everything they had.* With great power the apostles continued to testify to the resurrection of the Lord Jesus, and much grace was upon them all. There were no needy persons among them. For from time to time those who owned lands or houses sold them, brought the money from the sales and put it at the apostles' feet, and it was distributed to anyone as he had need (Acts 4:32-35).

Luke used this background to introduce Barnabas, the Son of Encouragement, who had sold a piece of property and had brought the proceeds to the apostles to be shared with those in need.

The first sin that distorted the idyllic lifestyle of the early church was, according to Luke, the love of money. Ananias and Sapphira sold a piece of property and were going to give all the proceeds to the church, but then decided to keep a portion of it for themselves. They lied to the church about the price, claiming

---

[15] The Greek word *koinonia* is not adequately conveyed by the modern connotation of *fellowship*. It is more correctly translated as *sharing* as seen by Luke's additional comments. See Lindy Scott, *Economic Koinonia within the Body of Christ* (Mexico: Editorial Kyrios, 1980) and Keith F. Nickle, *The Collection: A Study in Paul's Strategy*, Studies in Biblical Theology, no. 48 (Naperville, IL: Alec R. Allenson, 1966).

that the part they gave was the total price of the property. Their deceit was seen as a grave offense and resulted in their immediate and premature death (Acts 5:1-11).

Breaking the hold of Mammon means opening up your possessions to your neighbors in need. The New Testament reveals that our neighbors might not be geographically close to us. Luke tells the story of the Christian disciples in Antioch. When they heard about the hardships in Judea caused by a famine, they each according to their abilities sent money to meet the needs of the believers (Acts 11:27-30).

Nevertheless, the clearest example of international *koinonia* took place during the Apostle Paul's third missionary journey. Although Paul spent about five years in this journey, he apparently did not start many new churches. His main activity was the gathering of a collection from the young Gentile churches which would be taken to the impoverished church in Jerusalem. Paul describes both his motivation and his goal in his Second Letter to the Corinthians. He had already written to the affluent church in Corinth regarding the collection (I Corinthians 16:1-4). He had urged them to set aside some money every Sunday so that when he arrived they would not have to scurry around to find money for the offering. The Corinthian church responded enthusiastically and promised Paul that they would give a large amount. As the weeks and months went by, they forgot about the collection. So, after a year and a half, Paul writes them again dedicating an extended passage to the collection.[16] He begins

---

[16] II Corinthians 8-9. On very few occasions did Paul dedicate two entire chapters to one single topic, thus showing the extreme importance that he placed upon this topic. For a more thorough analysis of the collection see Scott, *Economic Koinonia*, pp. 113-137.

with the example of the poor Macedonian churches that, in spite of their poverty, gave up to and beyond their ability. The Macedonian believers well understood that giving themselves to the Lord and sharing their meager possessions with their brothers and sisters in Jerusalem was a holistic, unified act.[17] Paul then mentions his co-worker Titus whom he has sent to the Corinthians to help them fulfill their promises. He urges them that in light of their abundance in faith, speech, knowledge, zeal, and love, they should also abound in this "grace of giving."[18] Paul then pulls out his most convincing example: the Lord Jesus himself. "For you know the grace of our Lord Jesus Christ, that though he was rich, yet for your sakes he became poor, so that you through his poverty might become rich." (II Corinthians 8:9). God Himself, when faced with the deep need of humanity, practiced *koinonia* and shared His own righteousness through his death on behalf of our unjust human race. Paul states his goal: "Our desire is not that others might be relieved while you are hard pressed, but that there might be *equality*. At the present time your plenty will supply what they need, so that in turn their plenty will supply what you need. Then there will be *equality*" (II Corinthians 8:13-14).

This Pauline goal of *koinonia* was also considered to be normative for the other New Testament writers. James denounced the Pharisaical "faith" present in some of the churches.

---

[17] Jesus' teaching in Matt. 25:31-46 immediately comes to mind where Jesus affirmed that the way we treat the "least of these" is in fact the way we treat Jesus himself.

[18] It is possible that Paul is using some irony here. The city of Corinth was quite affluent in this period. The church tended to be arrogant and boastful of its spiritual gifts. Paul is urging them to match their spiritual boasting with the practical sharing of their possessions.

What good is it, my brothers and sisters, if a man claims to have faith but has no deeds? Can such a faith save him? Suppose a brother or sister is without clothes and daily food. If one of you says to him, "Go, I wish you well; keep warm and well fed," but does nothing about his physical needs, what good is it? (James 2:14-16).

Religiosity without action is not genuine faith. Not all religious people who are actively involved in their churches are true followers of Jesus.

The Apostle John also noticed people in the churches who did not follow Jesus' teaching. Like James, he urged the Christians to practice *koinonia*. Jesus Christ was to be the measure.

This is how we know what love is: Jesus Christ laid down his life for us. And we ought to lay down our lives for our brothers and sisters. If anyone has material possessions and sees his brother in need, and closes his heart against him, how does the love of God abide in him? Little children, let us not love with word or with tongue, but in deed and truth (I John 3:16-18).

John also wrote what God had revealed to him on the island of Patmos. The letter to the church at Laodicea (Revelation 3:14-20) is of special importance for the theme of the idolatry of money. Outwardly the church was affluent, independent and self-sufficient: "I am rich. I have acquired wealth and do not need a thing." Nevertheless, the church at Laodicea had deceived itself. From God's point of view, they were wretched, pitiful, poor, blind and naked. Their love of money had blinded them to the truth. They no longer represented the God proclaimed by Jesus and, therefore, they were about to be vomited from his mouth.

The consistent message of Scripture is that materialism, the worship of money and possessions, is idolatry. It chokes the word so that there is no fruit. It blinds believers from truly seeing the world from God's perspective. It can even rob people of their souls. Has this idolatry penetrated the United States? Let us now take a sobering look at the current situation.

Has the United States really Lost its Soul?

A recent dialogue in the *Chicago Tribune* has clearly raised the issue of the spiritual state of the United States. On May 28, 2004, Pope John Paul II warned Catholic bishops in the American heartland not to let the flock stray amid the lure of materialism. The Pontiff evaluated America and Americans as having a "soulless vision of the world," one characterized by an excessive materialism and a drift away from their spiritual roots.[19] The Pope's comments were not new, for he had already stated his argument on many occasions. Back in 1991, the Pope lamented that American Catholic Christians were being molded by the capitalistic, materialistic culture on the United States. This had resulted in their individualistic self-love.[20] After his five-day visit to the United States in 1995, the Pope again pointed out the deadly materialism of the North American culture. Then in his final World Peace Day message of the 20th century, Pope John Paul II branded capitalism's child—materialistic consumerism—as an evil of the same stature as Marxism, Nazism and fascism.[21]

---

[19] "Pope despairs of America's 'soulless' vision" in the *Chicago Tribune*, May 29, 2004, p. 1.

[20] Arthur Jones, "Capitalist Materialism Won't Make It Through Needle's Eye" in the *National Catholic Reporter*, 28:4 (Nov. 15, 1991): 22.

[21] "Pope Names Free Market Failures" in the *National Catholic Reporter*, 35:10 (Jan. 8, 1999): 28.

Illinois Congressman Henry Hyde, the Chair of the Committee on International Relations, took issue with the Pontiff's most recent comments. Hyde, a practicing Roman Catholic, wrote a long editorial "The Generous Spirit that is Uniquely American" published by the *Tribune*. Hyde perceived North Americans to be totally opposite from the Pope's description. According to the congressman, the Pontiff was "absolutely wrong" in referring to the U.S. as "soulless" because Americans have "a persistent religiosity" and "high levels of attendance at formal religious services" and maintain "a widespread belief in a supreme being" in contrast with secular Europe.[22] The congressman then elaborated on American generosity.

> We have been blessed with enormous wealth, but what is too often overlooked is our unprecedentedly generous sharing of this blessing with others. It would take several pages of this newspaper to recount even a fraction of the resources that the United States has devoted toward alleviating the world's poverty and disease—resources unparalleled in scale and breadth by any other country or international organization.[23]

Here we have two distinct visions of the United States: the Pope's version of a society that has lost its way because it has lost its soul and Hyde's perception of a deeply generous people, whose generosity is the fruit of their religiosity. Which vision is more accurate? Has the United States gained the whole world and lost its soul? And if so, was it because the church in the United States had lost its saltiness?

---

[22] Henry Hyde, "The Generous Spirit that is Uniquely American" in the *Chicago Tribune*, June 9, 2004, p. 30.
[23] Ibid.

The Pope's accusation is serious. Before patients undergo surgery, they like to get "a second opinion." A good doctor would examine her patient very carefully, analyzing all possible symptoms and testing all the vital organs. What is the current health of Christianity in the United States, especially in its relationship to money? Has the dreaded idolatry of money infested the church? We will first examine how the North American church understands the place of money in its presentation of the gospel message. We will then diagnose the church and the country in relationship to generosity and business practices.

How Biblical
is the North American Gospel?

The idolatry of money is at least as common among us today as it was among Jews twenty centuries ago. Nevertheless, most of our contemporary presentations of the gospel minimize the necessity of repentance and ignore completely the idolatry of money. In the 1950s and 1960s many North American evangelicals attempted to express the gospel through certain formulas such as Campus Crusade for Christ's *Four Spiritual Laws*. These presentations stressed "accepting Jesus as Savior" but did not emphasize sufficiently the need to turn from sin. For example, the gospel presentation expressed in the *Four Spiritual Laws* urged people to experience the "wonderful plan for your life" that God offers. Although it did mention that sin had separated us from God, the booklet did not ask people to confess their sins, much less to produce "fruits of repentance." Equally serious was the fact that the idolatry of money was entirely omitted.[24]

Evangelism Explosion was another gospel methodology that was highly successful, especially among senior citizens nearing the end of their lives. It was developed by Dr. James Kennedy, Senior Pastor at the Presbyterian Church in Fort Lauderdale, Florida. It situated the gospel in what would happen after death. The recommended introduction to the presentation of the gospel was to inquire of the non-Christian, "If God were to ask you, 'Why should I let you into my heaven?' what would you say?" By emphasizing the forensic forgiveness of sins as the way to get into heaven upon death, the present ethical demands of the gospel of the Kingdom were reduced to almost nothing.

Because these gospel presentations are considered "highly successful" among North American evangelicals, many also consider them to be faithful expressions of God's gospel. In their attempt to contextualize the gospel for specific age groups, whether it is for the young person's desire for the "abundant life" or the older adult's concern for going to heaven upon death, these presentations have departed from the emphases seen in Scripture. They shift the attention from God and His reign to human happiness. At the time these evangelistic methods were

---

[24] *Ten Basic Steps toward Christian Maturity. Step 7: The Christian and Witnessing* (San Bernardino, CA: Campus Crusade for Christ, 1968) was a commonly used manual to help prepare college students to share the gospel with their peers, especially in how to use the *Four Spiritual Laws*. There was no mention of repentance from sin or of turning from the idolatry of money in the entire manual. Sin was described as an "attitude of indifference to God." The individualistic answer suggested by Campus Crusade is far removed from the actions of repentance and love towards one's neighbor that were demanded by John the Baptist.

becoming standard presentations for evangelicals in the United States, a straight talking young evangelist, Billy Graham, did diagnose the North American disease.

> We are rich in the things that perish, but poor in the things of the spirit. We are rich in gadgets, but poor in faith. We are rich in goods, but poor in grace. We are rich in know-how, but poor in character. We are rich in words, but poor in deeds. We say we are rich, but in God's estimate we are wretched, miserable, poor, blind, and naked.[25]

Over the past three decades the "health and wealth gospel" has made even greater departures from Biblical teaching. Proponents of this "prosperity gospel" have arisen in both pentecostal and non-pentecostal circles, but they have different characteristics. Pentecostal television evangelists are quite explicit in their teaching on prosperity. Representative leaders such as Kenneth Hagin and Kenneth Copeland teach that God wants His children to be materially rich. A typical message goes like this.

> God loves you (the TV evangelist shouts to his listening audience). He loves you and He wills for you to enjoy perfect health. And He wants you to be rich. After all, the cattle on a thousand hills belong to Him. Would an earthly millionaire make his own children eat poor food, wear shabby clothes, and ride in a broken-down family car? Of course not! Neither will your heavenly Father give you anything but the very best. What is the desire of your heart? Name it, claim it by

---

[25] From "Challenge to America" in the *Hour of Decision*, 1963. Quoted in Bill Adler, *The Wit and Wisdom of Billy Graham* (New York: Random House, 1967), p. 71. It is important to note that Billy Graham, even four decades ago, was equating North America with the apostate church of Laodicea in Revelation 3:14-22.

faith, and it is yours! Your heavenly Father has promised it.
It's right there in the Bible.[26]

While recognizing the possibly sincere intentions of those who
preach this message, the evangelical statesman Kenneth Kantzer
soberly identified this as a "perverted gospel" and a "heresy."

> The greatest evil of this perverted gospel centers in its
> complete reversal of biblical values. Wealth is not our goal....
> The Christian is not to set a high priority on the well-
> advertised creature comforts that twentieth-century America
> makes possible. *The abundance of things we possess is not
> the measure of our true success. What most Americans call
> success is in God's eyes our downfall.*[27]

Non-pentecostal Christianity tends to be more subtle in its
expression of the health and wealth gospel. Even when the
sermon content does not emphasize material possessions, the
nonverbal cues are powerful advertisements for the prosperity
gospel. Churches are typically evaluated by the size of their
membership, the luxuriousness of their buildings, and the salaries
of the pastoral staff. It is far too common that people are chosen
for leadership positions in our churches and Christian
organizations based more upon their "financial success" than
upon the characteristics laid out by the Apostle Paul.[28] It is
interesting to note that Paul's criteria required that candidates for

---

[26] Quoted by Kenneth Kantzer, "The Cut-rate Grace of a Health and
Wealth Gospel" in *Christianity Today* (June 14, 1985): 14.

[27] Ibid.

[28] I Timothy 3:1-10 and Titus 1:6-10. It is usually expected that board
members of Christian organizations in the United States not only give
thousands of dollars to the organization, but also connect the development
staff with their wealthy friends.

leadership must be "free from the love of money" and not "fond of sordid gain." In his farewell speech to the Ephesian leadership he reminded them that he had not coveted anyone's silver or gold or clothes, he had supported himself and his colleagues by the labor of his own hands, and he reminded them of our Lord's words, "It is better to give than to receive." (Acts 21:33-35)

Here again the evangelist Billy Graham warned his United States audience that "Christian religiosity" was not a guarantee of faithfulness to God. His accusation was serious: our hypocritical religiosity was abhorrent to God. If his diagnosis was fairly accurate then, how is our spiritual health today?

> What a picture of America today—worshiping other gods while giving lip service to the true and living God. I tell you, God is sick of it! I tell you that our false pretenses and our hypocrisy are a stench in the nostrils of God![29]

Are North Americans Generous?

Representative Hyde affirmed that the United States is internationally known to be a generous country. Most North Americans agree with him. Surveys show that more than two thirds of the U.S. population believes that the United States is more generous than other developed nations. Nevertheless, the figures show the opposite to be true. The United States ranks dead last (in percentage of GNP) among major donors of foreign aid.

---

[29] "God's Warning" in the *Hour of Decision*, 1957. Quoted in Bill Adler, *The Wit and Wisdom of Billy Graham* (New York: Random House, 1967), p. 102.

**Table 1—Estimated Official Development Assistance from
Industrialized Countries as Percentage of GNP (1993)**

1. Denmark	1.03	10. Australia	.35
2. Norway	1.01	11. Switzerland	.33
3. Sweden	.98	12. United Kingdom	.31
4. Netherlands	.82	13. Italy	.31
5. France	.63	14. Austria	.30
6. Finland	.46	15. Japan	.26
7. Canada	.45	16. New Zealand	.25
8. Belgium	.39	17. Ireland	.20
9. Germany	.37	18. United States	.15

Source: World Bank[30]

The North American government did demonstrate a much greater generosity immediately after World War II had ended. At the height of the Marshall Plan, which was designed to help in the rebuilding of devastated Europe, the U.S. gave 2.79 percent of its GNP as foreign aid. By 1960 the percentage given as foreign aid had slipped to .53 percent of GNP. By 1993 it had fallen to .15 percent, equivalent to only $37.70 per person.[31]

On an individual basis, the situation is not much better. Many churches teach that Christians should practice the tithe by giving ten percent of their income to the church and other ministries. The truth of the matter is that North American Christians give only 3% of their income to their churches and to other charities. The overwhelming majority of these donations are utilized within

---

[30] World Bank, *World Development Report 1995*, p. 196. Some might question the use of a percentage of GNP instead of total giving. Nevertheless, the percentage method seems more in line with Biblical teaching as seen by the widow's mite. See also II Corinthians 8:12.

[31] Ronald J. Sider, *Rich Christians in an Age of Hunger*, 4th ed. (Dallas: Word Publishing, 1997), pp. 31-32.

the United States for church buildings, pastoral staff salaries, youth ministries, etc. A very small portion of this money reaches the neediest people in the Two Thirds World. Ron Sider states that Christians throughout the world control 62% of the globe's wealth.[32] If that is true, then a loving heavenly Father must either be enraged or deeply distressed over our greed and indifference.

AIDS is the scourge and plague of our times. We could hope that North American Christians would respond generously to diminish this disease. Highly respected C. Everett Koop, ex Surgeon General and a committed evangelical Christian, has argued that this is the time for Christians to demonstrate their generosity. Nevertheless, he cites that only 3% of North American Christians give anything to this cause. He denounces this as a deplorable affront to God.[33]

Is the Bottom Line the Only Line?

A few years ago I attended a Christian academic conference. One of the speakers was a professor in California where she also owned a large fruit orchard. As we talked over dinner, I found out that she employed "illegal aliens" in her orchards. Furthermore, I discovered that she paid them less than the minimum wage. I asked her if she didn't feel bad about paying them such low wages. She answered that she had to pay them so little in order to compete with the other orchards in the region.

---

[32] "Rich Christians in an Age of Hunger: Revisited after Sixteen Years," Wheaton College CACE Forum, November 10, 1993 (videotape).

[33] "An Evening with C. Everett Koop," Wheaton College, April 4, 2002 (taped interview).

Her answer highlights the tragic reality of our day: the bottom line usually takes precedence over every other consideration.

Has North American lost its soul and compassion? Lou Dobbs is the anchor and managing editor of CNN's *Lou Dobbs Tonight*. He has a regular series on his television program called "Exporting America." His website contains a list of thousands of "U.S. companies either sending American jobs overseas, or choosing to employ cheap overseas labor, instead of American labor."[34] He repeatedly berates these companies for their lack of love and loyalty to the American worker. He really gets angry at North American corporations that receive government bids and, at the same time, maintain tax havens offshore in the Cayman Islands, Jamaica, and the Bahamas. Whether Lou Dobbs is ethically correct or not in criticizing these companies, the fact of the matter is that most corporations are following the god of efficiency, the god of greatest profits, the god of the bottom line. The overwhelming majority of shareholders never communicate ethical concerns to their corporations' boards of directors. Their most important concern is the increasing value of their investment.

Does our Materialism Lead Us into Sin?

The genius of capitalism is that it frees up humanity's creative juices to produce more and better goods for human need. At its best moments, capitalism has been a tool and a servant, bettering

---

[34] "Exporting America" downloaded from http://www.cnn.com/CNN/Programs/lou.dobbs.tonight/

human life. At its worst moments, it has permitted various abuses of workers, damaged the environment, and glorified Mammon. Recent events suggest that the abuses are overtaking the benefits: the profits are defeating the prophets.

With the Enron debacle, white-collar corporation sin has become well known. The misbehavior was multi-faceted. For example, in their desire to make more and more money, Enron leadership manipulated California's oil supplies to artificially drive up prices. Criminal charges have been leveled at twenty Enron executives. More than a hundred additional executives throughout corporate American have been criminally charged within the past three years. Ten have already begun serving time in prison.[35]

A recent event in Chicago illustrates what has become all too commonplace in the business world: deceit is utilized to increase profits. In June 2004 it was reported that the *Chicago Sun-Times* exaggerated its newspaper sales in order to charge advertisers more money. The love of money leads to lying.

This dark cloud may have a silver lining. Given the increasing moral decadence of the corporate world, MBA programs throughout the United States have incorporated required courses on Business Ethics into their programs. It is a sad commentary on the state of the North American church that, in general, evangelicals have not been at the forefront of this ethical reformation.

---

[35] "Corporate Crime Watch" downloaded on June 21, 2004 from http://www.cnn.com/CNN/Programs/lou.dobbs.tonight/. Downloaded on June 21, 2004.

Advertising: Money Spent to Convince Us that Jesus was Wrong about Possessions

Advertising can be a useful and honorable business tool when it provides the public with truthful information. But we know that businesses primarily utilize advertising so that customers will buy more of their products. The more products sold, the greater the profits. Jesus taught that "one's life does not consist in the abundance of one's possessions" (Luke 12:15). Billions and billions of dollars are spent every year on advertising, much of which is utilized "to convince us that Jesus was wrong about the abundance of possessions."[36] More money is spent in the United States on advertising than on all the public institutions of higher education.[37] If Jesus was right about possessions, then our society is losing its soul.

Wealth and the War in Iraq

As seen in the first chapter, Latin American evangelical leaders pointed out that economic gain was a not-so-hidden motivation behind the invasion of Iraq. They generally base their accusation on Scripture, but more specifically on concrete examples leading up to the war. Although the descriptions of wars in the Bible reveal greed as a principal cause, it is the Apostle James who provides the clearest teaching on the source of wars.

---

[36] Richard K. Taylor, "The Imperative of Economic De-Development," *The Other Side* 10:4 (July-August 1974): 17.

[37] Sider, *Rich Christians*, p. 21.

> What causes *wars* and fightings among you? Don't they come from your desires that battle within you? You want something but don't get it. You *kill* and covet, but you cannot have what you want.[38]

If Christians would take James' argument seriously, they would be well prepared to discern between the true motives of war and the multitude of false arguments that are proffered to convince the citizens of a country that their national goals are noble and worthy. Although it is sometimes difficult to see one's own inconsistencies, others perceive them quite easily. Latin Americans frequently suggest these two examples.

Many of the later arguments regarding the invasion of Iraq concentrated on bringing "democracy" to that troubled country. The stated goal was that the voice of the people would be heard, because the leaders would then be elected by a majority of the population. Nevertheless, this argument in favor of democracy seems hypocritical to many Latin Americans. On the eve of the invasion, the United States asked Turkey if its military bases could be utilized for the attack. According to polls, 94% of Turkey's citizens were against the invasion and against the North American use of their bases. With such a clear mandate, Turkey's government respected the wishes of its citizenry and therefore denied the U.S. military access to its bases. Democracy was functioning as it was intended. The will of the people was respected. Nevertheless, the United States offered the Parliament

---

[38] James 4:1-3. Many modern translations change the meaning of the text from "wars" between nations (*polemoi*) to "fights and quarrels" between individuals. In this way Christians are ill-prepared to identify the hedonistic greed that lies underneath many wars. They are then misled into believing "moral justifications" for what are truly "immoral wars."

of Turkey millions of dollars in an attempt to persuade them to go against the democratic will of their people and grant access to the U.S. military.

A similar kind of anti-democratic pressure took place between Mexico and the United States. In 2003 Mexico occupied one of the rotating seats on the United Nations Security Council. The proposal of England, Spain, and the United States asking for military authorization needed one more vote to obtain the super majority that was required. Mexico could have easily provided that vote. But 90% of Mexico's population was against the war. The Mexican Government correctly represented its people on this issue and would not approve the resolution. The United States Government applied heavy economic pressure upon Mexican President Vicente Fox to persuade him to vote against the expressed desires of his people. The pressure did not work. Democracy in Mexico won out.

Ethnocentric Patriotism in the Bible

Materialism and ethnocentric patriotism are similar idolatries. They frequently intertwine and can rightfully be considered as twins. In this section we will explore two varieties of ethnocentric patriotism in the Scriptures: the kind occasionally practiced by the Jews and the type that occurred among the Gentiles throughout the Roman Empire.

To begin with, it is important to distinguish between a healthy, natural love for those people and culture closest to us and an unhealthy, excessive ethnocentric patriotism or nationalism. When we cheer for the hometown sports team, or when we want our children to do well in life, or when we long for justice to reign in our country, we are expressing a healthy patriotism. Nevertheless, this can easily become distorted into an unhealthy self-righteousness, one-sided partisanship, or ethnocentric nationalism if it leads us to thinking more highly of ourselves than we should or if it leads us away from God's understanding of justice. Ethnocentric patriotism is the belief that one's own nation (or race, or culture, or religious group, etc.) is inherently better than all others. It tends to blind us from seeing our own sins and mistakes. It frequently makes us resistant to change, even to the point of being reactionary. Ethnocentric behavior is precisely the activity Jesus warned about when he told us not to attempt to take the speck out of someone else's eye while we have a log in our own (Matthew 7:3-5). The good news is that, through repentance and forgiveness, it truly is possible to take the log out of our own eye, that is, to overcome our ethnocentricity, and then be able to help remove the speck from our neighbor's eye.

As we have already seen, the Pharisees were lovers of money. They also practiced ethnocentric patriotism. They were present when John the Baptist gave his "fruits of repentance" sermon.[39] John anticipated their thoughts: "Do not suppose that you can say to yourselves, 'We have Abraham for our father;' for I say to you, that God is able from these stones to raise up children of Abraham." The Pharisees believed that as God's chosen people they had special privileges with Yahweh. John the Baptist corrected their misconceptions. He called them a "brood of vipers," a phrase with especially negative connotations for Jewish leaders in light of Genesis 3. Furthermore, he warned them that they were not exempt from God's just demands. The Pharisees,

---

[39] Matt. 3:7-11. Matthew's version makes the Pharisees, along with the Sadducees, the primary motive and audience for John's strong words.

just like other Jews (and like all of humanity), needed to produce "fruit in keeping with repentance." If they did not change and demonstrate true repentance, they would be cut down and thrown into the fire.

Jesus agreed with John regarding the Pharisees and their eventual state. He referred to them as a "plant which my heavenly Father did not plant" and "blind guides of the blind." In the end they would be rooted up or would fall into a pit (Matthew 15:13). Jesus later confirmed that the Pharisees had indeed rejected "God's purpose for themselves" because they did not produce the necessary fruit that was required by John the Baptist (Luke 7:29-30).

Jesus worked hard to overcome the ethnocentric prejudices of his day, even among his own disciples. The Jews of Judea were bitterly opposed to the Samaritans. The Jews considered them to be racially inferior and religiously outside of Yahweh's covenants. Jewish believers would go to great lengths to avoid even stepping onto Samaritan territory. On a trip to Galilee, Jesus intentionally led his disciples through Samaria so that he could begin to break down their multiple prejudices.[40] His encounter with the Samaritan woman led not only to her conversion, but also to the conversion of many Samaritans in her hometown. From being a woman of bad reputation, she was transformed into the godly evangelist, the heroine of the story. Jesus' disciples had to come to grips with this unpleasant truth: the Samaritans were just as responsive (or perhaps even more responsive) to the message of Jesus as were their fellow Jews.

---

[40] John 4:3-42, especially verse 4. Most Jews would cross over to the eastern side of the Jordan River to avoid going through Samaria.

On many occasions Jesus would make the Samaritans the heroes of the episode. When asked by a lawyer about who is our neighbor, Jesus told the parable of a man who was robbed and left for dead on the road to Jericho. A priest came by...and did nothing. A Levite walked by and likewise was apathetic. But a Samaritan walked by and had compassion on the victim, bandaged up his wounds, took him to an inn, and paid for his expenses. The Samaritan, the despised mixed-raced *mestizo*, was the epitome of God's loving servant.[41]

Even within the life of the early church, ethnocentric patriotism reared its ugly head. The community of faith provided food for the needy widows among them (Acts 6:1-6). The Jewish widows from Judea were well cared for. But the Hellenistic Jewish widows of the Dispersion, those who had spent much of their lives outside of Palestine, were neglected. They were treated as second-class citizens and considered to be inferior, perhaps both religiously and culturally. This favoritism of one group at the expense of another was rightfully denounced as a wrong that needed to be corrected.[42] The church took strong action by choosing seven Hellenistic Jewish men to oversee the entire food distribution program.

The Apostle Paul, before his conversion, was a Pharisee and was very zealous for his Jewish culture, tradition and religion. He interpreted the faith of the first Christians as a deviation from the Jewish faith, rather than its fulfillment. He was so committed to his

---

[41] Luke 10:25-37. See also Luke 17:11-19 where Jesus healed ten lepers. It was only the Samaritan leper who glorified God and thanked Jesus. He then heard Jesus' words, "Rise and go your way; your faith has made you well." The Samaritans also had their share of ethnocentric prejudices as Luke 9:52-53 makes clear.

[42] See James 2:9.

ethnocentric beliefs that he persecuted the Christians, causing many to be imprisoned and some to be put to death. By his own admission, Paul was a sincere persecutor of the church (Philippians 3:6). It took a dramatic encounter with the risen Christ to convince Paul of his misguided patriotic zeal (Acts 9:1-9).

The Apostle Peter also had to overcome his own racial and religious prejudices before he could be used by God to take the message to the Gentiles. When he was staying at the home of a tanner named Simon, he went up to the rooftop to pray, but fell into a trance. In a vision he was told three times to eat all kinds of "unclean" animals. When he protested a voice responded, "Do not call anything impure that God has made clean." At first he did not understand, but later he realized that God was extending salvation to the Gentiles. His response to Cornelius is a tremendous model for Christians who desire to overcome their ethnocentric patriotism: "You are well aware that it is against our law for a Jew to associate with a Gentile or visit him. But God has shown me that I should not call any man impure or unclean" (Acts 10:9-48). This vision of the equality of humanity springs from Peter's better understanding of the nature of God: "I now realize how true it is that *God does not show favoritism* but accepts people from every nation who fear him and do what is right" (Acts 10:34-35).

Paul's preaching of the gospel in the city of Philippi presents us with a clear connection between materialism and ethnocentric patriotism. One of the first converts was Lydia, a wealthy vendor of purple cloth, who opened her heart to God and her home to Paul and his colleagues.[43] Shortly thereafter, Paul encountered

---

[43] Acts 16:11-40. In the case of Lydia the power of God overcame the power of Mammon as she placed her possessions at the service of the gospel.

a slave-girl who, through the spirit of divination that possessed her, brought much profit to her masters by fortune telling. Paul expelled the evil spirit from her. Her masters were angry because their hope of profit was gone. Seizing Paul and Silas and dragging them before the authorities, they expressed their frustration in ethnocentric terms, "These men are Jews, and *they are throwing our city into an uproar by advocating customs unlawful for us Romans to accept or practice.*" (Acts 16:21). This was obviously a false accusation to hide the slave-owners' greed, but it temporarily achieved its purpose: Silas and Paul were flogged and placed in prison. Nevertheless, after an earthquake and the subsequent conversion of the jailer and his family, Paul and Silas were set free in the morning. On the basis of Roman law and his rights as a Roman citizen, Paul appealed to the magistrates to exonerate the Christian faith. The authorities complied. An important lesson can be learned from the Philippian experience: the emotional, illogical, "mob-mentality" arguments frequently associated with ethnocentric patriotism can be overcome by cool-headed logic that appeals to the best moral and legal virtues within any society.

The gospel's entrance into the city of Thessalonica shows us the tragic consequences that occur when a religious group enters into an unholy alliance with a government at odds with their practices. There was a substantial Jewish community in Thessalonica, large enough to support a synagogue. Paul's preaching of the gospel caused some Jews, some God-fearing Greeks, and some leading women of the city to convert to Christ. Other Jews, who did not believe Paul's message, formed a mob and set the city in an uproar. They dragged Jason and some new believers before the city authorities and shouted, "These men who have upset the world have come here also; and Jason has welcomed them, and they all act contrary to the decrees of

Caesar, saying that there is another king, Jesus" (Acts 17:1-9). It is indeed tragic that Jews, who affirmed that only Yahweh was Lord (*kyrios*), argued against Christianity by defending the Roman Empire and the Emperor's idolatrous claim to be the only king within the empire. The early church showed its courage by constantly affirming, "Jesus is Lord," thereby affirming Jesus' deity and at the same time dethroning Caesar's idolatrous pretensions.[44]

The clearest example of the twin idolatries of materialism and ethnocentric patriotism is found in the city of Ephesus (Acts 19:1-41). The Ephesians were followers of the goddess Artemis (=Diana). They were extremely proud of the temple of Artemis, which was considered one of the seven great wonders of the ancient world. Much of the city's economic livelihood depended upon the worship of Artemis: tourism, temple prostitution, sales of Artemis statues, etc. The proclamation of the gospel of the Kingdom of God had a powerful impact upon Ephesus and all of Asia Minor. As was his custom, Paul began preaching the Kingdom of God in the Jewish synagogue at Ephesus. His success brought about so much opposition that he had to transfer his base of operations to the school of Tyrannus. Two years of daily preaching enabled all in Asia Minor to hear the word of the Lord. Many Ephesians turned away from their practice of magic and turned to God. They burned their books of magic that had a value of fifty thousand pieces of silver. The real controversy occurred when many people turned away from the worship of Artemis and began following Jesus. Sales of the silver shrines of Artemis plummeted. Demetrius, a silversmith, convinced other

---

[44] Throughout the first century A.D., the Greek word *kyrios*, as a title, could only be used for the Roman Emperor.

craftsmen that their continued economic prosperity depended upon the downfall of Christianity. Then he added the argument of religious nationalism:

> Men, you know we receive a good income from this business. And you see and hear how this fellow Paul has convinced and led astray large numbers of people here in Ephesus and practically the whole province of Asia. He says that man-made gods are no gods at all. There is danger not only that our trade will lose its good name, but also that the temple of the great goddess Artemis will be discredited, and the goddess herself, who is worshiped throughout the province of Asia and the world, will be robbed of her divine majesty. (Acts 19:25-27)

Demetrius' exhortation achieved its desired effect. A mob gathered and shouted for over two hours, "Great is Artemis of the Ephesians." Through skillful diplomacy the city clerk was able to quiet and disperse the mob. The historian Luke has carefully revealed the true motives behind the uproar. Although Demetrius was concerned about his monetary profits, he stirred up his countrymen based upon their religious and patriotic zeal. His true motives were hidden to the superficial observers, but we the readers have glimpsed the truth as correctly perceived by Luke.

It is no coincidence that a few years later, the Apostle Paul would write to Timothy, a young church leader in Ephesus, "For *the love of money is the root of all evil.* Some people, eager for money, have wandered from the faith and pierced themselves with many griefs."[45] It was precisely in Ephesus where Paul had

---

[45] I Timothy 6:10. Most modern versions dilute the force of Paul's words, such as the NIV's "the love of money is *a* root of *all kinds of* evil." Nevertheless, the grammatical structure of this passage is identical to John

experienced firsthand the evil animosity stirred up by Demetrius' greed. The apostle warns Timothy that he should at least consider the possibility of greed as a principal cause of the evils in society, although it might not be readily apparent. Just as roots are not usually visible, greedy people will hide their avarice from the view of others. While nationalism is often the immediate cause behind wars, the deeper root is frequently greed.

Scriptures concur that ethnocentric patriotism is dangerous. By stirring up people's emotional commitment to their country or ethnic group, it works against the truth and justice of God. It allows emotional fever to trump the truth. It blinds people from considering the claims of the gospel. It is even dangerous for Christians because it can weaken their testimony by compromising their loyalty to God.

Ethnocentric Patriotism in the United States

Most people in the United States are ethnocentric, just like many humans all over the planet. Nevertheless, the ethnocentric patriotism of North Americans can be very dangerous if they equate the economic and military might of the United States with ethical superiority. Many people in the United States think that their nation is the greatest country the world has ever seen. This belief crosses political divisions: Republicans and Democrats alike think their country is superior to all. For example, President George Bush, Sr. declared February 3, 1991 as a national day of

---

1:1, where Christians correctly reject any attempt to allow that the definite article "the" be changed to the indefinite "a".

prayer on behalf of Operation Desert Storm. He reminded his countrymen of their obligation to the world:

> As one nation under God, we Americans are deeply mindful of both our dependence on the Almighty and our obligations as a people He has richly blessed.... Entrusted with the holy gift of freedom and allowed to prosper in its great light, *we have a responsibility to serve as a beacon to the world*–to use our strength and resources to help those suffering in the darkness of tyranny and repression.[46]

In 1991, then President Bill Clinton expressed similar sentiments on the eve of sending troops to Kosovo.

> The United States, as the largest and strongest country in the world at this moment–largest in economic terms and military terms–has *the unavoidable responsibility to lead in this increasingly interdependent world*, to try to help meet the challenges of this new era.[47]

Both Presidents, George Bush, Sr. and Bill Clinton, saw the United States as thrust into a leadership role in the world. Both reasoned that military and economic prowess had placed them as the world's leader in morality as well.

One of the most notable foundations of North American ethnocentric patriotism has been civil religion. The lack of a state church in the early history of the United States facilitated the growth of a generally Protestant country with a fairly ambiguous

---

[46] Quoted in Roberta Coles, "Manifest Destiny Adapted for 1990's War Discourse: Mission and Destiny Intertwined" in *Sociology of Religion* 63:4 (Winter 2002): 403-426.

[47] Ibid.

God.[48] North American culture is filled with Judeo-Christian symbols. United States coins and bills in circulation affirm, "In God We Trust." Each President swears upon the Bible at the inauguration in Washington, D.C. "God Bless America" is widely sung throughout the country. Boy Scouts and Girl Scouts promote their "God and Country" merit badges as if every religion and patriotism were natural allies walking together hand in hand.

The Pledge of Allegiance is a clear example of this civil (and possibly not so civil) religion. On June 14, 2004, the Supreme Court did not rule the "one nation under God" phrase to be unconstitutional. Therefore the phrase could remain, at least temporarily, in the pledge. Every time that school children or adults recite this pledge, they affirm that God and the United States are integrally united. Obedience to one entity, by association, implies obedience to the other. By affirming that the country already demonstrates "liberty and justice for all" North Americans are lulled into believing that their country is almost sinless. This identification of God with country is further emphasized by the fact that men and boys are asked to remove their hats and caps when they recite the pledge. Men in the New Testament performed this same act when they prayed to God (I Corinthians 11:1-7).

Is pledging absolute allegiance to any country a Biblical concept? The Scriptures respond with a resounding "No!" Can we imagine the apostle John, having been exiled to the island of Patmos, pledging allegiance to the Roman Empire? Of course not! John likened that government to a beast that made war

---

[48] This can be seen in the deistic views of Washington and Jefferson.

against Christians and blasphemed God.[49] What about the apostle Paul? Wouldn't he, as a Roman citizen, pledge allegiance to the Roman Empire? Respect, yes. Allegiance, no! For Paul, governments were fallen institutions. He urged that all people, including government officials, the governors Felix and Festus, and even king Agrippa, should repent and turn from their sins and perform works worthy of justice.[50] It is the apostle Peter who explicitly taught how Christians should relate to their government (I Peter 2:17). He affirmed, "Honor the king." The verb that he used, "*timate*," means respect. It is precisely the same verb that he utilized earlier in the sentence, "honor all people." Far from exalting any government or giving it special allegiance, Peter urges us to treat all people with the same level of respect.

Christians in the New Testament were warned not to form entangling alliances that would compromise their allegiance to Jesus. Paul wrote, "Do not be unequally yoked with unbelievers, for what do justice and wickedness have in common?"[51]

---

[49] Revelation 13:1-10. Most commentators believe that John used the term "beast" to refer to the Roman Empire of his day, due to his phrase "authority over every tribe, people, language and nation." Even if the Roman Empire was merely the first in a long line of "beasts," which country today has that type of authority?

[50] Acts 24:1-26:32, especially 24:25 and 26:19-29. Even in the oft-quoted, and frequently misinterpreted, passage of Romans 13:1-7, Paul clearly affirms that human governments are *under* God and have to give an account to Him of their work as His servants (*diakonoi*).

[51] II Corinthians 6:14. Although this passage is commonly used to warn against marriages between Christians and those of other faiths, its original context was economic and political.

The War in Iraq and North American Ethnocentric Patriotism

During the war in Iraq, the activity of the Southern Baptist Convention has been the most ironic. Historically Southern Baptists have been staunch defenders of the separation between state and church.[52] In addition, the Southern Baptist Convention is an association of like-minded local congregations, in which each local church is quite autonomous. Therefore, it is difficult for the SBC leadership to speak on behalf of all of their churches, much less in the name of every member. Nevertheless, back in the early spring of 2003, the SBC President, James Draper, declared that the Baptists were in favor of the war in Iraq. More recently, on June 16, 2004, at their national convention in Indianapolis, the Convention reaffirmed their "pride and strong support for our American military." Even while they were demonstrating their support for United States soldiers fighting in Iraq, the Convention also discussed a proposal urging Southern Baptists to remove their children from the "godless" public schools in the United States.[53] It is truly bizarre that Baptist soldiers can kill in the name of the United States Government (and supposedly with the blessing of God) to protect and defend

---

[52] See Robert M. Calhoon, "Separation of Church and State" in *Eerdmans' Handbook to Christianity in America* (Grand Rapids: Eerdmans, 1983), pp. 271-273.

[53] Richard N. Ostling, "Baptists Reject Proposed Pullout from Public Schools" in the *Chicago Tribune*, June 17, 2004, p. 21. Although this resolution was eventually rejected, it is interesting to note that it was proposed by T.C. Pinckney, a retired Air Force General and Baptist delegate to the Convention.

the "American Way of Life" that supports a "godless" school system!

The issue of the war in Iraq has caused a serious separation to occur between the Southern Baptist Convention and the World Baptist Alliance which represents 210 national Baptist denominations with a total membership of 47 millions baptized believers. On March 24, 2003, the World Baptist Alliance condemned the invasion of Iraq as "a great sin."[54] Because the SBC President had already come out in defense of the war, the WBA's denunciation was seen as "theological liberalism." At their annual convention a few months later, the Southern Baptists appointed a commission to evaluate the situation. The commission recommended the separation of the SBC from the World Baptist Alliance. On February 17, 2004, the executive committee of the SBC voted to approve their recommendation. The SBC at their annual convention voted to formalize the separation accusing the WBA of theological liberalism, tolerance of homosexuality, support of the ordination of women pastors, and declarations against the United States. The WBA President, Korean Pastor Billy Kim, and the General Secretary Denton Lotz, responded to each of these accusations.[55] It is clear that the real issue was the SBC support for the war in Iraq. The WBA declaration affirmed, "We believe that Baptists should be good, patriotic citizens, but *patriotism should always be limited and judged by the Biblical call of our loyalty to Christ*, which is above

---

[54] *"Fraternidad Teológica Latinoamericana y Alianza Bautista Mundial rechazan la guerra"* en *Servicio de Noticias ALC*: March 25, 2003.

[55] *"Alianza Bautista Mundial rechaza imputaciones de la Convención Bautista del Sur"* en *Servicio de Noticias ALC*: June 22, 2004.

all."[56] It should be a serious warning to Southern Baptists in the United States when their fellow Baptists around the world are almost unanimous in their condemnation of the war in Iraq. Are the Southern Baptists the only Baptist Christians who are correctly interpreting the voice of the Lord or have they been misguided by their own ethnocentrism?

On several occasions President Bush asked rhetorical questions that expressed the sincere, but naïve, feeling shared by many of his countrymen: "Why does the world hate us? If we are so generous, so good, promoters of democracy around the world, etc., why do so many people hate us?" His own answer suggested that the hatred sprung from envy or rivalry or from the fact that the news media distort the goodness of the American people. He challenged the media moguls to do a better job of "getting our message out."

On the day sovereignty was transferred to the Iraqis, three North American marines were killed in a roadside bomb explosion. Another marine was interviewed about the situation and was asked what motivated him to be in Iraq. He responded, "We're just here to help the Iraqis. I don't know why the Arabs hate us so much."[57] President Bush and the unidentified soldier expressed the prevalent conviction that their country has been an unqualified positive force for good in the world. Perhaps many North Americans are sincere, but the Bible does warn us that sincerity is not a good measure of true justice: "The heart is deceitful above all things, and desperately corrupt, who can

---

[56] Ibid.

[57] Unidentified U.S. marine interviewed on *BBC World News*, June 28, 2004.

understand it?" and therefore the Lord will judge each person "according to the fruit of one's deeds."[58]

Soulful or Soulless?

We began this chapter by looking at two idolatries prevalent in Scripture: materialism and ethnocentric patriotism. Have these idolatries caused the churches in the United States to lose their soul? Decades ago the evangelist Billy Graham called the church to examine its predicament and come back to God. His words are even more timely today.

> Many men transformed themselves into gods and began worshiping themselves in their own power. During the past generation it has been *an appalling idolatry*, and its consequences have been two World Wars and the terrifying possibility of a hydrogen-bomb war.... *America, in trying to gain the world, has come very close to losing her own soul.*[59]

Eisenhower's Warning Comes True

In his last days of office, Republican President General Dwight Eisenhower issued a strong warning to the United States population. He explained the rationale behind the incredible

---

[58] Jeremiah 17:9-10. It is important to remember that much of Jeremiah's ministry involved pointing out the sin of God's people who did not wish to admit it.

[59] From "Americanism" in the *Hour of Decision*, 1956. Quoted in Bill Adler, *The Wit and Wisdom of Billy Graham* (New York: Random House, 1967), p. 79.

growth of a permanent *military-industrial complex*. Although its existence had been necessary, its continual growth and permanence posed a potential problem of gigantic proportions.

> We have been compelled to create a permanent armaments industry of vast proportions. Added to this, three and a half million men and women are directly engaged in the defense establishment. We annually spend on military security more than the net income of all United States corporations.[60]

Eisenhower feared that this military-industrial complex, in combination with military research dominated by the Federal government, would become the tail that would wag the dog. He urged his countrymen to become an "alert and knowledgeable citizenry" that could keep the complex in check.

President Eisenhower looked forward to a future with a vision for peace and equality.

> Down the long lane of history yet to be written America knows that this world of ours, ever growing smaller, must avoid becoming a community of dreadful fear and hate, and be, instead, a proud confederation of mutual trust and respect. Such a confederation must be one of equals. The weakest must come to the conference table with the same confidence as do we.[61]

---

[60] Dwight D. Eisenhower, "The Military-Industrial Complex" in Russell F. Weigley, ed. *The American Military: Readings in the History of the Military in American Society* (Reading, MA: Addison-Wesley, 1969), p. 155. On this issue Eisenhower and Martin Luther King, Jr. agreed. In a 1967 speech Dr. King declared, "A nation that spends more on weapons of destruction than on programs for social uplift is a nation approaching spiritual death."

[61] Ibid., p. 157.

Sadly, Ike's fear of a growing military-industrial complex, combining the twin idolatries of materialism and ethnocentric patriotism, has won the day. His vision of a more humble United States that would promote mutual trust and respect among equal nations has evaporated. Latin American countries, as well as most nations throughout the world, have noted sadly the increasing going-it-alone and bullying attitude of the United States (as illustrated by the North American refusal to participate in the Kyoto accord, nuclear disarmament agreements, etc.).

In summary, the twin idolatries of materialism and ethnocentric patriotism are rivals of the Lord Jesus Christ. These idolatries are prevalent in the United States culture and government and have also made inroads into the North American church. This has produced a Manichaean vision of the world where one side is totally right and the other is totally wrong:

> Who is not with us is against us. Who does not support the policies of the President is on the side of the terrorists. The mission of the United States is to free the world of the evil and the perversity of the terrorists.[62]

---

[62] Quoted by veteran evangelical missionary in Latin America, John Stam, *"El presidente Bush es un peligro para el mundo, dice teólogo estadounidense"* in *Servicios de Noticias ALC*: October 2, 2003. Because President Bush did not heed the advice of the Pope, of ex-President Carter, nor of the United Nations, and because he would not even receive the Methodist Bishops who tried to dissuade him from waging war on Iraq, Stam notes that the President is unwilling even to listen to respected Christian leaders. Stam concludes that President Bush either does not know Biblical social ethics or that he is a heretic regarding Christian ethics.

The practice of the Christian religion in the United States has been distorted, just like the Pharisaical distortion of Judaism. Therefore, Christianity in the United State has been utilized to justify a non-Christian position regarding the war in Iraq. In the next chapter we will explore steps to take in order to return to God's ways.

5

A Plea for Responsible Christian Reflection and Action

He has showed you, O man, what is good.
And what does the Lord require of you?
To act justly and to love mercy and to walk humbly with your God.
(Micah 6:8)

At the memorable International Congress on World Evangelization held in Lausanne, Switzerland, thirty years ago, evangelical Christians recognized the socio-political dimensions of their mission in the world. According to *The Lausanne Covenant,*

> We affirm that God is both the Creator and Judge of all men. We therefore share his concern for justice and reconciliation throughout human society and for the liberation of men from every kind of oppression. Because mankind is made in the image of God, every person, regardless of race, religion, color, culture, class, sex or age, has an intrinsic dignity because of which he should be respected and served, not exploited. Here too we express penitence both for our neglect and for having sometimes regarded evangelism and social concern as mutually exclusive. Although reconciliation with man is not reconciliation with God, nor is social action

evangelism, nor is political liberation salvation, nevertheless we affirm that evangelism and socio-political involvement are both part of our Christian duty. For both are necessary expressions of our doctrines of God and man, our love for our neighbor and our obedience to Jesus Christ. The message of salvation implies also a message of judgment upon every form of alienation, oppression and discrimination, and we should not be afraid to denounce evil and injustice wherever they exist. . . . The salvation we claim should be transforming us in the totality of our personal and social responsibilities. Faith without works is dead. (Paragraph 5)[1]

The relevance of this call to socio-political responsibility on the part of Christians can hardly be exaggerated. Who can deny the rampant "alienation, oppression and discrimination" that characterize today's world under the dominion of the global capitalist system? Who can remain indifferent to the plight of millions and millions of people totally unable to satisfy their basic needs, while at the opposite end a very small minority of the world population are living extravagant lives and continue to pile up wealth for themselves? From a biblical perspective, we Christians are called to share God's "concern for justice and reconciliation throughout human society and for the liberation of men from every kind of oppression." We are called to be witnesses to God's Kingdom of love and justice. How can we be silent in the face of the drama of hunger, misery and squalor all over the world? How can we remain complacent with a system

---

[1] See "The Lausanne Covenant" in *Let the Earth Hear His Voice*, edited by J. D. Douglas (Minneapolis: World Wide Publications, 1975), pp. 3-9. Cf. John Stott, "The Lausanne Covenant With an Exposition and Commentary," *Making Christ Known* (Carlisle, Cumbria: Paternoster Press, 1996), pp. 1-55.

that pays lip service to democracy and freedom but subjects people everywhere to slavery to economic totalitarianism?

With these questions in mind, we would propose that what the Kingdom demands at this critical moment in the history of humankind is nothing less than a revolution of values for the recovery of justice and peace, a new spirituality that brings together worship and public life, and a restructuring of the Church for sacrificial service to the gospel of Jesus Christ.

I. A Revolution of Values

The extent to which the "Righteous Kingdom" (Martin Marty) has lost the very notion of righteousness is indicated by the way in which, since 9/11, the "war on terrorism" has become the basis for justifying U. S. state terrorism and an open violation of human rights. Convinced that in the 1970s the Vietnam war was not lost in Vietnam but in the United States because of the lack of public support to the war, U. S. government officials have made it their aim to persuade people in that nation, *by every possible means*, that the greatest threat to modern civilization is terrorism and that, consequently, U. S. foreign policy has to be defined in terms of the war on terrorism. Sad to say, the first victim of this kind of strategy is truth. Truth is sacrificed on the altar of propaganda. As a result, people give their consent to a foreign policy that has no respect for ethics nor for the lives of thousands and tens of thousands of defenseless people in the countries where that policy is applied, be it Guatemala in the 1950s, Nicaragua in the 1980s, or Iraq in 2003.

This special effort to win the minds and hearts of the citizenry through propaganda is compounded by a wide acceptance of the "American Way of Life" and its inordinate consumption on the part the large majority of people in the United States. A powerful corporate elite controls the political and military complex. Very few people, however, bother to raise questions on the effects that the policies adopted and the decisions made by the managers of the most powerful empire history has ever known may have on the poor at home or abroad. The consumer is satisfied to reap the benefits of the empire's growth, and that contributes to the stability of the system. From the perspective of the Kingdom of God, the "fundamental principles" of the affluent society, such as materialism, ethnocentrism, and individualism, must be questioned for the sake of justice and peace. And they must be questioned wherever they appear, in the North or in the South. The real threat to modern civilization in general and to the United States in particular is not terrorism but a system of institutionalized injustice which benefits the wealthy and oppresses the poor. In Orlando Costas' words, "the poor's right to life must be defended and the machinery of socioeconomic oppression and repression that contributes to poverty must be fought."[2]

Justice as a Condition for Peace

Peace, involving security, is a desirable end for both individuals and nations. The human heart longs for peace. Peace therefore imposes itself as a primary political objective which no responsible government can overlook. Whether in the East or in the West, the North or the South, the prophetic vision of a world in which swords will be beaten into ploughshares and spears into pruning hooks finds a positive response. Peace, however, has its

---

[2] *Christ Outside the Gate: Mission Beyond Christendom* (Maryknoll, N. Y.: Orbis Books, 1982), p. 61.

own conditions. Unless these are fulfilled, the ideal of peace is nothing but wishful thinking. Isaiah 32:17 points to the main condition for peace: justice. It reads: "The fruit of justice (*sedeqah*) will be peace (*shalom*); the effect of justice will be quietness and security forever." In other words, peace is related to justice as a fruit to the tree that produces it. Where there is no justice, there can be no peace. Injustice and peace cannot coexist. As Christopher D. Marshall has put it:

> The central concern of biblical law was the creation of *shalom*, a state of soundness or "all rightness" within the community. The law provided a pattern for living in covenant, for living in *shalom*. Specific laws were considered just, not because they corresponded to some abstract ethical norm or reflected the will of the king or protected the welfare of the state, but because they sustained *shalom* within the community. This, in view of Israel's origins as liberated slaves, necessarily required provisions for the impoverished and oppressed, which is why so much of biblical legislation is devoted to "social justice" concerns, such as care for widows, orphans, aliens and the poor, the remission of debts, the manumission of slaves, and the protection of land rights. In this connection, covenant justice could be understood as positive succor for, and intervention on behalf of, the poor and the oppressed.[3]

The prophet Isaiah speaks out of a context of injustice and oppression. The ruling classes have become corrupt and are using their power to exploit the poor. They are "rebels, companions of thieves; they all love bribes and chase after gifts"

---

[3] *Beyond Retribution: A New Testament Vision for Justice, Crime, and Punishment* (Grand Rapids, MI: Wm. B. Eerdmans Publishing Co., 2001), p. 48.

(Is 1:23). Their God-given task is to seek justice, to encourage the oppressed, to defend the cause of the fatherless, to plead the cause of the widow (cf. Is 1:17). Instead, they are busy looking after their own selfish interests, adding house to house and field to field as if they were living alone in the land (cf. Is 5:8). They have replaced justice with bloodshed, and righteousness with cries of distress (cf. Is 5:7). Through unjust laws and oppressive decrees, the poor are deprived of their rights, the widows are exploited, the fatherless are robbed (cf. Is 10:1, 2). And no justice is to be expected from the judicial system because of "those who with a word make a man out to be guilty, who ensnare the defender in court and with false testimony deprive the innocent of justice" (Is 29:21).

Injustice is the order of the day. Yet injustice does not come alone. Where justice is disregarded, anarchy breaks in. "People will oppress each other—man against man, neighbor against neighbor. The young will rise against the old, the base against the honorable" (Is 3:5). Law and order are essential to the well-being of any society. But when law and order are invoked so as to defend vested interests, lawlessness and disorder are unleashed and the moral foundations of society are destroyed. Law and order used as rationalizations to justify the oppressors inevitably lose all respect from the oppressed–the victims of the system which invokes them. Ethical values are then increasingly ignored. The situation that emerges is that which the prophet suggests when he says: "Woe to those who call evil good and good evil, who put darkness for light and light for darkness, who put bitter for sweet and sweet for bitter" (Is 5.20). All sense of right and wrong is lost. As a result, social chaos takes over.

To complicate the picture even more, in Isaiah's day the people of Israel are quite complacent in their sin. The prophet's message of God's judgment falls on deaf ears. Because of their rebellion, says the prophet, Assyria, a godless nation, will be used as a rod of God's anger; because of their lack of understanding, they will go into exile, "their men of rank will die of hunger and their masses will be parched with thirst" (Is 5:13). His warning, however, is met with indifference and scorn. The sound of destruction is in the air, but instead of repentance and sackcloth there is joy and revelry, eating and drinking. "Let us eat and drink," they say, "for tomorrow we die" (Is 22:13). Hedonism goes hand in hand with false security. The false security of the leaders of Israel in Isaiah's day is expressed in confidence in the military power of Egypt. Rather than repenting and waiting upon the God of justice, they have made an alliance with Pharaoh, forgetting that "the Egyptians are men and not God; their horses are flesh and not spirit" (Is 31:3). What a warning to those who even today seek peace and security by means of naked force but show no concern for justice!

The Prophetic Vision of Peace

Chapter 32 of Isaiah begins with a promise of a kingdom where "a king will reign in righteousness and rulers will rule with justice" (v. 1). In contrast with the situation of institutionalized violence in Jerusalem, in that kingdom to come the fool will no longer be called noble, nor the scoundrel be highly respected; the hungry will not be left empty, nor will the thirsty go without water, nor will the poor be destroyed when his or her plea is just (vv. 5-8). Jerusalem is about to be destroyed. The complacent women who live in it, therefore, are exhorted to give up their false security and to recognize their plight (vv. 9-13).

After this exhortation the prophet turns his eyes to the changes which are going to take place once God's judgment is fulfilled.

The Spirit of God, says he, will be poured out and a new creation and a new society will come into existence. Then, "righteousness will dwell in the desert and justice live in the fertile land. The fruit of justice (*sedaqah*) will be peace (*shalom*); the effect of justice will be quietness and confidence forever. My people will live in peaceful dwelling places, in secure homes, in undisturbed places of rest. Though hail flattens the forest and the city is leveled completely, how blessed you will be, sowing your seed by every stream, and letting your oxen and donkeys range free" (vv. 16-17).

This prophetic vision of a world of peace is best understood in contrast with the chaotic situation described before. The peace here referred to is no mere absence of war, but *shalom*, that is, harmony, well-being, wholeness, abundance, prosperity, health, happiness, fulfillment both for the individual and for society. In our text it is related to tranquility, quietness or rest and to confidence, security or safety. Surrounded by a situation marked by injustice as well as by social tension and insecurity, the prophet envisions a new era in the history of his nation. The description of this new era is cast in words which remind us of the year of Jubilee according to Leviticus 25: "In the year of Jubilee everyone is to return to his own property... Do not take advantage of each other, but fear God. I am the Lord your God. Follow my decrees and be careful to obey my laws, and you will live in safety in the land. Then the land will yield its fruit, and you will eat your fill and live there in safety" (vv. 13, 17-19). The link that Isaiah sees between justice and peace, between obedience to God's laws and safety, is already made in the ancient revelation given to Moses on Mount Sinai, according to tradition.

When Justice Reigns

The longing for a world in which men and women can enjoy life in all its dimensions, undisturbed by violence and misfortune, is a common characteristic of humankind. It is not surprising, therefore, that the promise of peace and security is frequently an important aspect of political rhetoric everywhere. Our text, however, in line with Mosaic revelation, places justice and peace in a relationship of cause and effect: "the fruit (or work) of justice will be peace."

The justice of which the prophet speaks is nothing less than God's justice–the justice that he loves and that he wills; not merely a social convention or a human value, but a divine charge, God's demand. And it is closely associated with compassion for the oppressed and the powerless, the socially marginalized and the weak. It is a "bias toward the poor". It has to do with God's concern for the needy and disenfranchised. Because God is a God of justice, it is sinful to remain indifferent to the situation of people who suffer from causes beyond their control.

Justice is an essential condition for the existence of *shalom*. No justice, no peace! Justice and peace are inseparable; they are united in marriage and their marriage cannot be destroyed. In the words of a psalmist, "love and faithfulness meet together; justice and peace kiss each other" (Ps 85:10).

Peace Without Justice?

In the absence of justice only a counterfeit peace is possible: the false security of the oppressors, based on coercion, or the slumber of the oppressed, based on fear, but not real peace. The peace of a cemetery, a concentration camp, or a country under military occupation, but not genuine, lasting peace. *Shalom* can never be the experience of a corrupt society that uses religion to legitimize private interests. Of a materialistic society obsessed with wealth and indifferent to the plight of the poor. Of a hedonistic society oriented towards the satisfaction of artificially-created needs and blind to the suffering of the masses. Of a consumer society committed to the idolatry of the fashionable and callous to the misery of the underprivileged. Of a wasteful society given to the ideology of unrestrained economic growth and heartless in the face of the hungry multitudes.

Nor can *shalom* be a reality in a world characterized by international socioeconomic injustice. A world dominated by the lust for political power and oblivious to human rights. A world in which bread is taken out of the mouth of the deprived masses in order to fatten an already overfed elite. A world in which the future generations of the poor nations are economically mortgaged by the rich. The only peace possible in this kind of world is the peace imposed by a terrorist state. A peace built on bloodshed. A sham peace especially designed for the wealthy, privileged elite, but bought with the lives of the oppressed. A false peace that the poor abhor and the rich cannot fully enjoy. A peace that threatens to blow up modern civilization.

If the fruit of justice is peace, the fruit of injustice is violence and social chaos, enmity and insecurity, hatred and fear. Every injustice committed against the poor carries with it the seeds of subversion. Justice leads to life, injustice ends in death. Injustice not merely violates human rights, but it is a sin against the living God, who loves justice. Therefore, those who persist in injustice place themselves under the judgment of God. "He who mocks the poor shows contempt for their Maker; whoever gloats over disaster will not go unpunished" (Prov 17:5).

It follows that the most efficient way to work against peace is to work for injustice, and the most efficient way to work for peace is to work for justice. Sow injustice and you will reap violence. Sow justice and you will reap peace. As someone has put it,

"Those who make peaceful revolution impossible, make violent revolution inevitable."

From this point of view, the first Kingdom priority today is a revolution of values–a revolution which will place justice above security and peace above economic gain. The passive accommodation to the "American Way of Life" is cooperation with the "international dictatorship of economic power" (Helder Camara) and a sad enslavement to the principalities and powers of this world. Acquiescence with the "war on terrorism" in the name of national security is inimical to faith in the Prince of Peace. The support of a foreign policy that favors vested interests in the name of economic development is contrary to God's will, for he requires "to act justly and to love mercy and to walk humbly" before him (Micah 6:8).

The prophetic denunciation of every form of injustice and exploitation is an essential aspect of the Christian witness. Where that denunciation is absent from the Christian witness, the Church is unfaithful to God and lacks the authority to proclaim the Good News to the poor. As Dom Helder Camara has put it, "Woe to Christianity on the day the eyes of the masses are opened, if they believe themselves to have been abandoned to the great and powerful with the connivance of the Church."[4]

In practical terms, this revolution requires, in the first place, *a process of "conscientization"* of Christians regarding both the ethical demands of the Kingdom and the socioeconomic and political situation of the world. Those of us who confess Jesus Christ as our Lord have been given the possibility of experiencing the Kingdom of justice and peace that he inaugurated in his

---

[4] *Revolution Through Peace* (New York: Harper Colophon Books, 1971), p. 104.

coming. All of us should perceive the possibility to live out that reality in the midst of a world of injustice and oppression. The need is for a contextual exposition of Scripture to open up these possibilities before the People of God with prophetic passion and pastoral concern.

Conscientization is needed by both the rich and the poor. The rich need to see their relation to the poor from a totally different angle. They need to see that what is required of them is far more than mere assistance to the poor. What is required of them is justice, and that involves empowering the weak so that they may be able not only to cover their basic needs but to fulfill their God-given vocation as human beings. On the other hand, the poor need to be liberated from fatalism and to recover a sense of their own human dignity. Both rich and poor need to learn the meaning of creative cooperation in transforming reality for the sake of *shalom* for the whole of humankind.

The revolution of values requires, in the second place, *a process of cross-fertilization* between Christians from various nations, cultures, and social strata. In Jesus Christ, all the barriers that separate human beings have been broken down. We Christians should, therefore, avail ourselves of every opportunity to establish meaningful relationships with people (especially the poor and marginalized) who will help us experience the reality of the Kingdom from a different angle and to see things from "the underside of history."

The revolution of values requires, finally *a process of transformation*, both personal and communal, by the power of the Spirit. The new humanity created in Christ is being shaped in history as the humanity that reflects his character and embodies the values of the Kingdom. Christians should be open to the action of the life-giving Spirit and obedient to his leading.

In the final analysis, the revolution of values is the work of the Spirit through his Word and the Christian community. Although it finds its nucleus in the Church as the community of the Kingdom, it points beyond the Church to God's intention to create a new world of justice and peace. And no one can guess what God may do through a minority that confesses Jesus Christ as Lord and lives by the power of that confession.

II. A New Spirituality

The second priority for the missionary agenda of the Church is a spirituality that will help Christians to draw on the resources provided by the Spirit of God to become agents of justice and peace in every area of life.

The subtle temptation to separate religion from ethics seems to be part and parcel of human life. When recognized, it helps to understand how it can happen that individual piety, expressed in terms of church attendance, Bible study, and prayer, can be combined in the same person with a total disregard for justice. In that case, spirituality is understood in terms of religious acts, but it has no, or very little, incidence on the way the religious person relates to his or her fellow human beings. God's response to this kind of spirituality is eloquently described in Isaiah 58.

According to this passage, the people of Israel have been complaining that God is indifferent to their fasting. "'Why have we fasted,' they say, 'and you have not seen it? Why have we humbled ourselves, and you have not noticed?'" (v. 3) A solemn religious act is not working! God's answer through the prophet leaves no room for doubt that the real problem is not on God's but on people's side: their religion has been separated from ethics. Their fasting is combined with quarreling and strife (v. 4). Spirituality has been reduced to a religious act, a means to manipulate God in order to obtain his favor, without any regard for God's justice. That is ritualistic religion and it stands in contrast with the kind of "fasting" that God has chosen: "to loose the chains of injustice and untie the cords of the yoke. . . to share your food with the hungry and to provide the poor wanderer with shelter—when you see the naked, to clothe him, and not to turn away from your own flesh and blood." (vv. 6-7). Religion void of justice is sham spirituality.

From a Christian perspective spirituality has both personal and social dimensions. It is inextricably related to the fulfillment of God's purpose for human life. At the very heart of the gospel of the Kingdom is God's intention to create a new world where people are reconciled to him and to one another through Jesus Christ. A gospel that conveys the idea that salvation is a subjective experience of isolated individuals is not the Christian gospel. This is not to deny the importance of conversion and the need for personal commitment. It is, rather, to affirm that being "born again" is far more than an individualistic religious experience. If anyone is in Christ, there and then God's new world becomes visible–a new creation encompassing heaven and earth is manifest. Forgiveness of sin and God`s call to become his "fellow workers" go together. Worship and public life are inseparable.

If the fruits of the gospel are to be made evident in today's world, far more attention will have to be given to the need for a new spirituality that combines prayer and praxis and enables Christians to be in the world the salt, the light and the leaven of the Kingdom. This kind of spirituality is not merely for "the chosen few" who are willing to dedicate themselves to "full-time

Christian service," but for all the people of God, regardless of their occupation or station in life.

There is a deep socioeconomic and political crisis in the world today. The imbalance of power between the so-called developed countries, including the United States, and the rest of the world has produced a situation of injustice and poverty which is no longer sustainable. In the final analysis, there is here a *spiritual and ethical* problem. That being the case, the Christian mission in this distressed world calls for a creative minority that embodies the ethics of the Kingdom, lives by the power of the age to come, and invites people to leave their old ways and to believe that in Jesus Christ the new creation has broken into history for the healing of the nations.

III. Restructuring of the Church

Finally, if the Church is to be used by the Spirit as God's witness to justice and peace, she must restructure herself for the mission of the Kingdom. Like Christ, the Servant-King, she does not exist for herself but for others. She, like her Lord, has been sent "to preach good news to the poor", "to proclaim freedom for the prisoners and recovery of sight to the blind, to release the oppressed, to proclaim the year of the Lord's favor" (Lk. 4.18-19). Her life and mission derive their meaning from this overarching purpose, and her structures are in place when they facilitate the fulfillment of her God-given vocation.

Accordingly, the Church in the Two-thirds world cannot simply adapt herself to the oppressive colonial structures of society. Nor can the Church in the First world in general and in the United States in particular allow herself to become a corporation that accepts the logic of death of the military-industrial-political complex. Nor can her missionary and service agencies simply be modeled on the transnational corporations with their criteria for productivity, efficiency and success.

Perhaps the greatest challenge posed to the churches in the United States today is how to witness to the Kingdom of love and justice in the midst of a society in which "the socially scripted role as self-interested consumer forms the center and ground of all value, the goal of all activities and relationships" and "individuals hearken to whatever promises to provide them with the 'choices' that will satisfy their self-directed appetites."[5]

Orlando Costas did well in insisting that if the Church is to be faithful to her call, she has to learn to go with Christ "Outside the Gate" and to engage herself in "Mission Beyond Christendom". In other words, she has to renounce every temptation to become established, accepted, and acceptable to the power holders. She has to take the side of the powerless and marginalized, and organize herself accordingly for her mission of *shalom*. Costas saw in this area one of the basic problems of the Christian mission. In the face of "an amorphous community with very shallow rootage in the gospel of Christ," he called for "healthy growth"—"a process of holistic development in which the community of faith is fed by new *members*, expands the participation of its members within its *organic* life, deepens its *understanding* of the faith, and becomes an *incarnated* servant in

[5] James V. Brownson, Inagrace T. Dietterich, Barry A. Harvey, and Chales C. West, *Storm Front:The Good News of God* (Grand Rapids, MI: Wm. B. Eerdmans Publishing Co., 2003), p. 5.

its social situation."[6] This was his way of saying that the Church does not exist to promote a private religious experience which will assure everlasting life by virtue of "cheap grace," but to enlist people for the service of the Kingdom of justice and peace.

One of the most encouraging signs of the Church's renewal in Latin America in the 1970s and 1980s was the growth of the *comunidades eclesiales de base* ("grassroots ecclesial communities"). This is not the place to elaborate on the subject, but a few comments on it are unavoidable in relation to the restructuring of the Church for mission. As a matter of fact, these communities that emerged as the new model for the Church in several countries, especially in Brazil, were fundamentally a new articulation of the Church for the mission of the Kingdom in a context of poverty and oppression. Often defined as "the Church of the poor and from the poor," they functioned side by side with other popular organizations involved in the struggle for justice. Perhaps more significant from the point of view of Protestant Christianity, however, was the fact that they rediscovered the meaning of the priesthood of all believers. In contrast with traditional Roman Catholic theology, they viewed all Christians as equal members in the body of Christ and, in line with this, believed that all Christians had a part in the Christian mission. In Leonardo Boff's words,

> The mission of the People of God is not entrusted only to a few but is given to all; sacred power is, initially, held by everyone and only later is held by sacred ministers. All are sent out to proclaim the good news about the bright future of history and about the meaning of the world already won and

---

[6] Op. cit., p. 97.

anticipated by the resurrection that makes Jesus' utopic truth about the Kingdom real and concrete.[7]

Sadly, this vision of the Church has to a large extent disappeared under the pressures of the Vatican. At least in Latin America, the Roman Catholic Church lost what might have been her last opportunity for wholesome renewal. The *comunidades eclesiales de base* movement, however, lasted long enough to show the realizable potential of an alternative way to be a faith community made up of common people committed to Jesus' call to his disciples, to be "the salt of the earth" and "the light of the world."

Could it not be that what wealthy white churches in the United States need in order to release all their potential for the mission of the Kingdom is to follow the same pathway as that of "the Church of the poor and from the poor"? The answer, however, is that they cannot unless they are willing to divest themselves of their special privileges and to break free from the military-industrial-political complex that enslaves them. They need to break free from it and to place themselves at the service of the hungry, the thirsty, the stranger, the naked, the sick, the imprisoned. Without that, they simply reflect the self-serving culture and the power of the American empire—the "Empire Lite," as Michael Ignatieff has called it[8]—but fall far short of the demands of Kingdom.

---

[7] *Church: Charism & Power. Liberation Theology and the Institutional Church* (New York: Crossword, 1984), p. 155.

[8] *Empire Lite* (London: Vintage, 2003).

Conclusion

The history of the Church provides plenty of evidence to show that the people of God cannot fulfill their prophetic role in relation to socioeconomic and political realities without paying a cost–indeed, a *very high* cost sometimes. This should not surprise anyone who is familiar enough with Jesus' warning to his disciples: "Blessed are you when people insult you and falsely say all kinds of evil against you because of me. Rejoice and be glad, because great is your reward in heaven, for in the same way they persecuted the prophets who were before you" (Mt 5:11-12). This beatitude, however, seems to be irrelevant to people who have grown accustomed to the idea that they live in a "Christian country" where religious freedom is guaranteed. Is this not one of the blessings of Christendom?

Let us remember, however, what happened in another "Christian country" in the last century: Germany. By no means was Hitler an unpopular political leader! For all practical purposes National Socialism became the ideology of the large majority of people. Even among theology professors and pastors, only a small minority had the courage to go against the stream. The Third Reich was regarded as a "terrorist organization" and "race and national tradition" became the slogan of the day. Nazism had a blinding effect to the extent that the Pastors' Emergency League could draw up statements such as the following:

> Yes, "praise God, all ye lands!" – "for around us" is emerging "the national awakening of folk and land" which bears witness to the fact "we are still a young nation." . . . praise God, "we" Christians "love our nation as our mother." And

we have a "government that agrees with and protects the soliarity of Christendom and national tradition" which is our destiny and the "indispensable prerequisite" for the "outer rise and inner well-being" of the nation.[9]

Contrast this pledge of allegiance with the Theological Declaration of Barmen, drafted by Karl Barth and issued by the Confessing Church in May, 1934:

> We reject the false doctrine, as though the church could and would have to acknowledge as a source of its proclamation, apart from and besides this one Word of God, still other events and powers, figures and truths, as God's revelation.
> We reject the false doctrine, as though there were areas of our life in which we would not belong to Jesus Christ, but to other lords. . . .
> We reject the false doctrine, as though the church were permitted to abandon the form of its message and order to its own pleasure or to change in prevailing ideological and political convictions. . . .
> We reject the false doctrine, as though the State, ever and beyond its special commission, should and could become the single totalitarian order of human life.[10]

Evangelical churches in the United States, under the government of President George W. Bush, are at a crossroads. Our plea is for responsible Christian reflection and action. With Dietrich Bonhoeffer, who was sentenced to death in a Nazi

---

[9] Quoted by Frank Jehle, *Ever Against the Stream: The Politics of Karl Barth, 1906-1968* (Grand Rapids, MI: Wm. B,. Eerdmans Publishing Co., 2002), p. 51.

[10] Ibid.

concentration camp, we believe that "while being able to forget may be a blessing, memory, the repetition of lessons we have received, is yet a part of responsible life."[11] And Christian discipleship involves fully responsible life.

---

[11] *I Loved This People* (London: S. P. C. K.), p. 17.

APENDIX I

Fear

Fear. I felt fear. For the first time since my now-distant childhood, I felt really afraid when the President of the United States, after carrying out his "preemptive strike" against Iraq, said that Syria had better watch out, that Iran had better watch out, that Cuba and whatever other country on earth that threatens its interests had better watch out.

Fear of the United States? Fear of those who brought us the gospel, of the ones who taught us values like respect for human rights, of those who with their tithes built churches, seminaries, hospitals, and schools?

With gratitude I remember the phenomenal contribution that that great North American leader Martin Luther King, Jr. made to humanity with his "I have a dream" speech and with his peaceful resistance on behalf of human rights. I also remember with gratitude the U. S. president Jimmy Carter, now the winner of the Nobel Peace Prize, one of the few who denounced and confronted the military dictatorship that from 1976 to 1983 made more than 30,000 Argentines "disappear." And I also recall the revolution of the 1960s and the popular resistance to the Vietnam War.

All these things I remember, and I ask myself, "Fear of my friends, fear of my Christian brothers and sisters?"

We know that every nation has the legitimate right to defense and security, and I'm aware that since September 11, 2001, you all carry around a new fear (other fears were already dancing around you: fear of unemployment [I think that in the USA it's around 6%], fear of losing the "American way of life," fear of repeating Oklahoma City). But now a new fear has taken up residence. You all are now afraid of international terrorism. As strange as it may seem, the very country of democracy and individual rights turns out to produce in a large percentage of humanity the same feeling international terrorism produces: fear.

Thousands of North Americans are upset at the possibility of new restrictive measures and extreme security precautions taken up with reticence by a country in which the citizen, accustomed to living with the concept of "total freedom," feels more and more trapped between a multitude of security measures and the fear that the officials have turned into a doctrine.

The dictionary defines terrorism as "domination by means of terror. A succession of violent acts executed to instill terror," and defines terror as "fear, fright, horror of an evil that threatens or of a danger of which one is afraid." Terrorism is, then, a strategy of domination that utilizes the fear of others. The only ones free from terrorism are the terrorists themselves because they have been trained not to feel fear and because they feel omnipotent and seemingly unconcerned about a suicide attack or an attack from the Pentagon.

Ever since the United States invaded Iraq as a preventive measure, we have been afraid. It is with this fear that I, and a large part of your population, feel that I propose to start out my reflections. I confess that they arise from the subjective logic of the emotions, or from my gut, and that as such they do not offer many answers to the questions that rationality poses. But these propositions are no less valid because of this. Neither does cold rationality answer the questions of the heart. I also confess that I'm neither an economist nor a politician, but I believe that, as a pastor, I ought to share with you what I feel.

I also warn you that I'm not anti-Yankee. I confess that I've always felt respect and admiration for your people; I also confess that one time I was tempted to leave for that Mecca of the modern western world. But today, from my internal world, I feel that the U. S. represents the greatest threat to world peace. And I am afraid.

It is not only President Bush's threats that awaken terror. There are other threats that come to us from the North, threats that inspire terror equal to that of an armed invasion.

We are afraid every time the International Monetary Fund demands new austerity plans that affect retired people, teachers, or hospitals. We are afraid when they insist we deepen the neoliberal economic prescriptions that, after 20 years of application, have only made the poor poorer and the rich richer. We were afraid when they gave us millions of dollars in credit even though they knew that our Criollo politicians were corrupt and inept spendthrifts (our governments are no better than yours) and that in the long run the debt would be paid with the hunger of the people.

We are afraid when the market "god" and an astute publicity apparatus force us towards a consumer society in which if you don't consume, especially at a determined level, you're a nobody; you don't exist.

We are afraid of the intellectual terrorism of one of your prophets, Francis Fukuyama, when he presents to us the democratic neoliberal model as the only possible model; it is the model towards which all the nations on earth are peacefully marching because it is the only model that lasts, with no other alternatives, because history has already shut out those who want other options.

We are afraid when acting contrary to the Bible becomes the method of defending the Bible, manipulating texts that legitimate holy war or that justify invasion.

Our manufacturers are afraid when they go out to compete in the international market where globalization preaches free trade on the one hand but on the other hand allows protectionism and subsidies for products coming from the dominant countries.

We are afraid, to the point of stupor, when they keep asking us to wait for the fulfillment of the prophecy of trickle-down economics: first we have to wait for those on top to get richer because later there will be so much abundance that those on the bottom will begin to benefit. No one forgets the consequences of the neoliberal policies of the 1990s: social deterioration, unemployment, debt, "development" in reverse, and the painful migration of our young people to other countries. Do we have to keep waiting for the trickle-down theory to finally kick in?

We were afraid of getting used to the horrors of warfare when from a comfortable armchair we went flipping through the channels looking for the most "realistic" images of the war.

We were afraid at the weakness of the United Nations that couldn't stop the invasion of Iraq. If the only international space for resolving conflicts through peaceful diplomacy and negotiation was unable to detain the war-like escalation, now who is left to do it the day that the United States perceives us as a threat to its interests?

I wouldn't say that these acts are terrorism, but they are forms of creating fear. They aren't acts of terrorism as spectacular as what the newspapers and television were showing on September 11, but they are equally tragic and atrocious because they are equally devastating in terms of human victims.

How do we get out of this vicious cycle of violence and terror? How do you all get healed from the fear of terrorism, and how do we who are not terrorists get healed from fearing intimidation from the country that has achieved the greatest military power in history? I invite you all to a few generalizations that nevertheless have the virtue of making us think.

In the first place, you all will be here in our country for a few days to get to know a different reality. That is the first little step. Knowing the reality of the poor and walking in their shoes even for a little while is the beginning of change. In the parable of the Good Samaritan, only one man stopped to face the reality on the road; the other two continued on with their planned activities. Maybe they even thought, "That happened to him because he wasn't in the temple like we were." But one man stopped before the reality of the fallen man and changed his scheduled activities. We need to let the reality of those fallen from the system impact us, and we need to change our agendas from band-aid plans to genuine programs for transforming reality.

Another step towards getting over the fear is changing our lifestyles. We need to reorient our habits of consumption. Something is wrong when, in visiting someone's house or inviting someone to my house, I'm ashamed because of the inequality between our standards of living. Something is wrong when in one country 31% of the population is obese and in another country 30% of the population consists of malnourished children. We don't need to wander through the immense sea of merchandise at Wal-Mart, agitated and anxious to fill our carts with trifles. We don't need new and powerful cars to make ourselves feel strong and happy; we don't need eggs cooked in three different ways (fried, scrambled, or omelets), cereal, sausage, pancakes, oatmeal, cream, juice, fruit, bacon, and mountains of butter (nor do the Argentines need so much meat at their barbeques). It's worth asking the question, "What hole are we trying to fill when the compulsion to buy dominates us? Is it just our stomachs?"

To overcome our fear, we need to participate in critical thinking. It is said that you all are too gullible towards those who govern you (you're not alone; many Argentines also believed the dictator Galtieri when he led us into war with England over the Falkland / Malvinas Islands). If that's the case, you need to recover some critical thinking. Think, reflect, be suspicious, ask questions, investigate, research and raise doubts. Don't believe naively the first thing that the political discourse or the media tell us. For example, up to now the chemical and biological weapons, for which the war on Iraq was apparently started, haven't shown up. If we had used critical thinking Bush probably wouldn't have had 70% of the United States population in favor of the war, according to the polls.

To overcome fear it is necessary that justice be built on a foundation of peace and not under the threat of force. There is no peace without justice. And one indication of justice would be less poverty in the world. Today 45% of the world's population lives on less than two dollars a day, and one billion, two hundred million people live below the poverty line. The peacemakers ought to work for justice and equity. Fear will never leave the world while the economic programs of the powerful countries don't take into consideration the need for human solidarity and a commitment to international social justice.

To get over our fears we have to consider that at their most basic level all these fears deal with ethical questions of right and wrong. We can't make our fears leave us while we continue believing that the end justifies the means. The fears won't disappear from among us unless we replace the ethics of pragmatism and utilitarianism as our basis for decision-making. Every ethic that violates the dignity of the human being or the validity of human rights, that justifies indiscriminate force, or that encourages distrust between human beings generates power for a few but fear for the rest.

Even if all these propositions lean towards utopianism, we shouldn't allow the cynicism of the "realists" to rob us of our dreams and hopes for a world without fear. If these roads are not the way, others will have to open up where now there are none. But we should not relinquish the belief that a different world, a world without fear or poverty, is possible.

Before going on to some of your questions that may have arisen from these reflections, I want to leave you all with some of my questions to get you thinking as you go.

- Do you all think that the poor are poor because they didn't figure out how to take advantage of the opportunities the system gave them?

- Do you believe that the United States is a nation specially chosen by God to defend freedom in the world?

Which would be your priority in the use of your resources, to fight against terrorism or to fight against poverty?

- Why is the typical family in the United States today afraid of international terrorism but the typical Norwegian family is not?

- Do you believe a change in the worldwide market system and a reorientation of globalization are necessary? The international market in money and financial products is 100 times greater than the total of the international market in real goods (why would you open a factory, give people jobs, and produce goods if you could make easy money without lifting a finger?).

- Do you believe the state ought to intervene in social policies like health care, education, and human rights?

- Should the economy be at the service of humanity or humanity at the service of the economy?

- Do you believe that the principles of the first Puritan colonizers, principles like living simply, saving, and austerity, ought to be practiced and defended today as much as individual liberties should be?

The world is a little ship in which we all travel together. We all depend on some essential provisions like air and water. If one of them grows scarce, all of us would be afraid, and sooner or later all of us would perish. Justice and peace are also essential elements in our little earth-boat. If we work hard to create them for the future, the fear that today governs both all of you and us will only be a memory of a past that will never return.

Thank you for visiting us. Thank you for listening to these still somewhat-disorganized ideas. Thank you for the small services you are offering in our country. Thank you for helping us not to fear you.

Jorge Galli
Buenos Aires, Argentina; June 2003

APENDIX II

Theology and Implications of Radical Discipleship[1]

A number of issues have thrust themselves upon us from papers delivered in this Congress and, from the subsequent wrestling with them under the authority of God's Word, a number of us have felt the compulsion of his Spirit to share this response.

We affirm that . . .

The *evangel* is God's Good News in Jesus Christ; it is Good News of the reign he proclaimed and embodies; of God's mission of love to restore the world to wholeness through the Cross of Christ and him alone; of his victory over the demonic powers of destruction and death; of his Lordship over the entire universe; it is Good News of a new creation of a new humanity, a new birth through him by his life-giving Spirit; of the gifts of the messianic reign contained in Jesus and mediated through him by his spirit; of the charismatic community empowered to embody

---

[1] This document was the result of meetings held by an *ad hoc* group that was spontaneously formed by "young Evangelicals" at the beginning of the International Congress on World Evangelization (Lausanne, Switzerland, July 16-25, 1974). The language, which some might consider sexist, reflects the 1974 setting.

his reign of shalom here and now before the whole creation and make his Good News seen and known. It is Good News of liberation, of restoration, of wholeness, and of salvation that is personal, social, global and cosmic. Jesus is Lord! Alleluia! Let the earth hear his voice!

The *communication of the evangel* in its fullness to every person worldwide is a mandate of the Lord Jesus to his community. There is no biblical dichotomy between the Word spoken and the Word make visible in the lives of God's people. Men will look as they listen and what they see must be at one with what they hear. The Christian community must chatter, discuss and proclaim the Gospel; it must express the Gospel in its life as the new society, in its sacrificial service of others as a genuine expression of God's love, in its prophetic exposing and opposing of all demonic forces that deny the Lordship of Christ and keep men less than fully human; in its pursuit of real justice for all men; in its responsible and caring trusteeship of God's creation and its resources.

There are times when our communication may be by attitude and action only, and times when the spoken Word will stand alone; but we must repudiate as demonic the attempt to drive a wedge between evangelism and social action.

The *response demanded by the evangel* is that men and women repent of their sin and every other lordship than that of Jesus Christ, and commit themselves to him to serve him in the world. Men are not already reconciled to God and simply awaiting the realization of it. Nor can biblical authority be found for the false hope of universalism; the reality of the eternal destruction of evil and all who cling to it must be solemnly affirmed, however humbly agnostic the Bible requires us to be about its nature.

Salvation is by God's grace on the sole ground of Christ's death and resurrection and is received by obedient faith. Repentance is demanded; men must experience a change of understanding, attitude and orientation. But the new birth is not merely a subjective experience of forgiveness. It is a placement within the messianic community, God's new order which exists as a sign of God's reign to be consummated at the end of the age.

Methods in evangelization must center in Jesus Christ who took our humanity, our frailty, our death and gave himself in suffering servanthood for others. He sends his community into the world, as the Father sent him, to identify and agonize with men, to renounce status and demonic power, and to give itself in selfless service of others for God. Those who proclaim the Cross must be continually marked by the Cross. With unashamed commitment to Jesus Christ we must *engage* in the mutual listening of dialogue, the reward of which is understanding. We need to meet men on their own ground and be particularly attentive to the powerless. We must use the language, thought-forms and imagery appropriate to differing cultures. As Christians, we must live in such unity and love that men may believe. We must allow God to make visible in the new humanity the quality of life that reflects Christ and demonstrates his reign. We must respect cultural integrity while being free from all that denies or distorts the Lordship of Christ. God's Spirit overcomes all barriers of race, color and culture.

Strategy for world evangelization in our generation is with God, from whom we eagerly anticipate the renewal of his community, equipping us with love and power so that the whole Christian community may make known the whole Gospel to the whole man throughout the whole world. We believe God to be calling us into greater unity and partnership throughout the earth to fulfill the commission of our Lord Jesus Christ.

We confess that . . .

We have been failing in our obedience to the Lordship of Christ and have been refusing to submit to his Word and be led by his Spirit.

We have failed to incarnate the Gospel and to come to men as servants for Christ's sake.

Our testimony has often been marred by triumphalism and arrogance, by lack of faith in God and by diminished love for his people.

We have often been in bondage to a particular culture and sought to spread it in the name of Jesus.

We have not been aware of when we have debased and distorted the Gospel by acceptance of a contrary value system.

We have been partisan in our condemnation of totalitarianism and violence and have failed to condemn society and institutionalized sin, especially that of racism.

We have sometimes so identified ourselves with particular political systems that the Gospel has been compromised and the prophetic voice muted.

We have frequently denied the rights and neglected the cries of the underprivileged and those struggling for freedom and justice.

We have often separated Jesus Christ the Savior from Jesus Christ the Lord.

We have sometimes distorted the biblical understanding of man as a total being and have courted an unbiblical dualism.

We have insulated new Christians from life in the world and given simplistic responses to complex problems.

We have sometimes manipulated our message, used pressure techniques and been unduly pre-occupied with statistics.

We have allowed eagerness for qualitative growth to render us silent about the whole counsel of God. We have been usurping God's Holy Spirit of love and power.

We rejoice . . .

In our membership by his Spirit in the Body of Christ and in the joy and love he has given us in each other.

In the openness and honesty with which we have met each other and have experienced mutual acceptance and forgiveness.

In the possibilities for men to read his Word in their own languages through indigenous translations.

In the stimulation of mind and challenge to action that has come to us from his Word as we have placed the needs of our generation under its judgment and light.

In the prophetic voices of our brothers and sisters in this Congress, with whom we go forth in humility and hope.

In the certainty that the kingdoms of this world shall become the Kingdom of our God and of his Christ. He shall reign forever. Alleluia!

We resolve . . .

To submit ourselves afresh to the Word of God and to the leading of his Spirit, to pray and work together for the renewal of his community as the expression of his reign, to participate in God's mission to his world in our generation, showing forth Jesus as Lord and Savior, and calling on all men everywhere to repent, to submit to the Lordship, to know his salvation, to identify in him with the oppressed and work for the liberation of all men and women in his name.

LET THE EARTH HEAR HIS VOICE!

Printed by
Roberto Grancharoff e hijos
Tapalqué 5868, Buenos Aires, Argentina
Te. 54-11-4683-1405

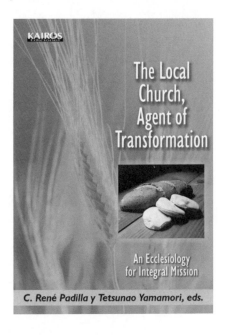